H   H   H

PCS TO CORPORATE AMERI   for
the military officer and is the mc   ket
today for any officer considering a ~~permanent~~ change of station to
the business world.

PCS TO CORPORATE AMERICA was written by Roger Cameron,
one of the originators of JMO recruiting and co-owner of the
premier JMO recruiting firm, Cameron-Brooks, Inc. For over
three decades, Roger has helped officers make successful transitions to the business world.

PCS TO CORPORATE AMERICA, Roger, and Cameron-Brooks
are recognized worldwide as the authority on career transitions.
Spotlighted on CNN and all major network affiliates, Roger has
also received acclaim in publications including *FORTUNE*, *The
Wall Street Journal* and *The Stars and Stripes*.

PCS TO CORPORATE AMERICA combines over three decades
of experience in one career reference handbook. There is no other
source of information available on the market today which provides the wealth of information contained in just this one book.

PCS TO CORPORATE AMERICA explains what to expect
during the entire career search process—from resume guidelines,
interview preparation, strategy, and techniques, through the
follow-up process, accepting a job offer and and starting your
new business career.

PCS TO CORPORATE AMERICA provides the tools for success
in a corporate interview and future business career. It will give
any officer a foundation for world-class interview preparation
and set him or her on a path for a world-class business career.

H   H   H   H   H   H

*"**PCS** superbly taught me how to communicate the valuable traits I gained as a military officer in terms that Corporate America could understand. I am convinced that there is no better way to prepare yourself to leave a military career than through the processes that Roger eloquently illustrates in his book. **PCS** anecdotes that the greatest truths come in small packages!"*

— Carl Herberger
Senior Project Manager
Campbell Soup Company

*"**PCS** improves with age. As a former candidate turned recruiter, I see the value of Roger's lessons repeatedly. It should be your primary resource in preparing for any professional interview, regardless of your background. **PCS** is not a one-time read. If your copy is not completely highlighted and book-marked by the time you are ready to interview, you have bypassed a key learning opportunity. Applying every aspect of the book is critical to your success."*

— Scott A. Milliren
Manager, Systems Development
Helmerich & Payne International Drilling Co.

*"Roger's book mirrors his organization and the process of placing JMOs in Corporate America. Not a word is placed without careful thought and clear purpose. Not a minute spent reading is without focus on the opportunity ahead and how to make the most of it. No JMO who is even remotely considering leaving the military can read this book too early. **PCS** will enhance every step of preparation, every minute of the career search and every day of your new career."*

— Dave Burggren
Branch Manager
Carrier Corporation

*"**PCS** is about learning how to communicate your unique experiences into successful business terms. Invest the time to study this book. **PCS** is not about tricks, gimmicks, or clever answers. This book is about helping you know and represent yourself such that a company will invite you to the next step in the interview process."*

— Andee Hidalgo
Vice President, Institutional Sales
US Bancorp Piper Jaffray

*"**PCS** is an excellent resource for any junior officer making a transition to Corporate America. The book guides you through the process using simple, real-life examples based on Roger's decades of experience."*

— Ross Beaton
Project Manager
Vast Solutions, a division of PageNet, Inc.

"If you are leaving the military for Corporate America, read Roger's book! Roger has set a standard for preparing junior military officers to enter the business world that no one else has come close to matching."
— David Edmonds
  Executive Vice President and Human Resources Director
  AmSouth Bank

"Roger drills you on what works, what doesn't work, and gives you that much needed confidence boost. In PCS, Roger provides the knowledge, skills and attitude in proper balance. Don't kid yourself, failure to prepare is obvious and limits your possibilities. Master this book, listen to Roger and make being prepared second nature."
— Tom Anderson
  Marketing Director
  Ethicon Endo-Surgery, a division of Johnson & Johnson

"PCS is a must-read. It is a straight-forward, no-nonsense guide to what you have to do to prepare and successfully execute a transition to the corporate world. Applying what Roger says will make a transition seem easy! Read it before you talk to Roger or decide to leave the military, and then re-read it. You will benefit even if you decide to stay in."
— Aaron Dahnke
  Strategic Planning Manager
  E&J Gallo Winery

"As a paratrooper, I had to trust my parachute before I could calmly exit the aircraft. As an aviator I had to trust my aircraft before I could fly. Having faith in the BEST equipment was key to my success in the military. As a JMO departing the military, PCS to Corporate America was the equipment I most relied on to ensure my success. Thanks to Roger and his advice, I landed a career with a company that almost exclusively recruits from Top 10 MBA schools."
— James "Chip" Clingham
  Brand Management
  Kraft Foods

"PCS to Corporate America is the best single reference I have found on interviewing, making a positive first impression and taking the ominous world of Corporate America by storm! Now that I am in the business world, I make sure that PCS is never further than an arm's reach away. The fact is, as I continue to meet more and more influential people, I find myself using many of the concepts presented in Roger's book. I firmly believe that the skills I learned from PCS have given me the edge for rapid advancement."
— Charlie Rizzo
  Equipment Engineering Leader
  Corning, Inc.

*"**PCS** was my bible for getting out of the Army. It helped me understand and prepare for some of the cultural differences I would be facing in the civilian world. Since starting my civilian career, I have used what I learned in **PCS** as a guide when conducting interviews for my company. I realize how lucky we are as JMOs to have this resource because the information in this book puts you far ahead of your civilian peers."*
— Martha C. Wehner
Consultant
Arthur Andersen

*"Long after my initial purchase, I still find myself referring to Roger's book. Daily, I find myself in some variation of an interview, where I am challenged to quickly and effectively communicate an idea and support the position with facts or personal experience. The tips contained in **PCS** help prepare people for just those situations. It is full of advice to help develop personal insight, improve communicative skills, manage challenging assignments, seek opportunities for broad personal growth, and maintain a reasonable work life balance."*
— John C. Sanchez
Business Sector Controller
Kimble Glass

*"Roger's wisdom and insight into the hiring mind is tremendous. Following Roger's guidance will improve your performance by a factor of 10. **PCS to Corporate America** is a great tool for anyone in the job market. It's a great handbook on how to land a great job and prosper in it."*
— Greg Bowman
Director, Facility and Supply Procurement
H.E.Butt Grocery Company

*"**PCS** is about modeling excellence in everything you do. Roger's advice is tremendous. Everything I do counts for or against me in Corporate America. The popularity contests of high school and college days are ancient history. Roger espouses the benefits of being professional, knowledgeable and articulate in every interaction. When you do this, the competition is likely to be left spinning in the wake, confused, but still 'cooler' than the person who just beat them. Model excellence, there is too much at stake to be cool."*
— Luke Lozier
Field Clinical Representative
Guidant Corporation

*"**PCS to Corporate America** gave us the foundation needed to transition successfully from the military to a FORTUNE 500 company. In **PCS**, Roger tells it like it is. The book set our expectation levels and increased our confidence in successfully engaging with individuals in the corporate world. **PCS** helped us make a lasting first impression and also taught us how to maintain it throughout our business careers."*

— Laura and George Hluck
Market Development Engineering Manager and Project Leader,
Information Technology (respectively)
Corning, Inc.

*"My journey into Corporate America started with Roger eight years ago when I read **PCS**. Today, I am 32 years old and running an $80 million open-heart surgery device business for a publicly traded company. Roger knows what he is talking about and what Corporate America is looking for—success! Those who have set and accomplished goals in high school, college and the military will continue to excel in the business world."*

— Pat Mackin
Vice President
Genzyme Surgical Products

*"**PCS** was the most influential part of my decision to exit the military. The book provided me with the knowledge and tools to transition to the business environment without skipping a beat. In **PCS**, Roger outlines those qualities that great leaders use in all arenas but combines the specific business expertise required to train you to become technically and tactically proficient for the corporate battlefield. I now refer to **PCS** as my career bible to keep me honest with my own development plan."*

— Mark Buck
Manager
Solectron Corporation

*"**PCS to Corporate America** and my association with Roger Cameron marked the turning point in my professional career. **PCS** prepared me for a move from the ordinary to a dream job and career. Many people have asked me how I managed to land such a great job right out of the military. The answer: **PCS** laid the groundwork and taught me to control my environment."*

— Beth Gulitus
Regional Business Director
Ethicon Endo-Surgery, a division of Johnson & Johnson

*"**PCS** is a remarkable enabler for the JMO striving for a career in Corporate America. It dispels the mystery of interviewing, offering critical guidance for a successful transition. Reading **PCS** gave me unshakeable confidence in my interviews. It can do the same for you!"*
> — Craig A. Williams
> Brand Management
> Kraft Foods

*"The most critical tool I had in transitioning from the military to Corporate America was **PCS**. The advice, guidance, and wisdom contained in this book was essential to my career transition. It not only prepared me for the transition from the military to Corporate America but it also provided the foundation for my success at Indigo. All individuals who desire to make a career transition should read and know this book well."*
> — Christopher Prentice
> Brachytherapy Specialist
> Indigo, a division of Johnson & Johnson

*"**PCS** is an excellent reference tool because it offers all of the advice and information you need for a successful transition to Corporate America. It is succinct and to the point—just simple no-nonsense lessons for success. **PCS** also continues to be useful after you enter the business world. Roger's lessons on communication, professionalism and attitude will always be crucial to your success in Corporate America."*
> — Corinne Johnson
> Mechanical Engineer
> Guidant Corporation

*"At some point in every officer's career, you are faced with the decision to stay or go. Before you make up your mind, read **PCS**. This book was a tremendous catalyst for me to start asking the right questions and thinking critically about my future. Don't rely on second hand information when your career hangs in the balance. Read **PCS** early in the decision-making process and make an informed decision based on quality research and real life experiences."*
> — Charlie O'Neil
> Content Production Manager
> pcOrder.com

*"In interviewing, as for any important inspection, tactical exam, or actual operation in the military, knowledge of the battlefield and preparation are the keys to success. **PCS** is the book that lays out the 'interviewing battlefield'. It will help you identify and avoid pitfalls and enable you to use aspects of the interviewing environment to your advantage. If you study it, apply the time-proven techniques, and utilize process discipline in your preparation, you are guaranteed to have career options open up and the ability to select the right career for you."*

— Bill Sheehy
Department Head, Equipment Engineering
Corning Asahi Video Products Co.

*"**PCS to Corporate America** is more than a guide for a transition to corporate employment. It is a mini-MBA course for officers who are considering leaving the service for Corporate America. The concepts Roger presents in **PCS** will make you a better performer—period. It made me a better officer in my last two years of service, and it prepared me for success in my new career. At Procter & Gamble, I work mostly alongside MBA graduates, and I can honestly say I have never felt at a disadvantage with respect to my peers. The principles in **PCS** are a roadmap for career success anywhere."*

— Randy Sadler
Brand Management
Procter & Gamble

*"The beauty of **PCS** is that it prepares candidates in every facet of their professional life. It helps candidates to know themselves and develop a long-term professional plan. As a result, you are not just thinking about what job you want and where you want to work today, but also about what and where you want to be tomorrow and how you will get there. I always ask candidates whom I interview (military and non-military) what their long-term professional objective is. Rarely do I find someone who knows. I hire the ones that do."*

— Kurt A. Bradtmueller
Group Marketing Manager
Westell Technologies

*"**PCS** gave me the tools I needed to earn top notch opportunities with top notch companies. Read and reread it again and again. Complete every exercise at least three times. Be disciplined and you will not be sorry. I am proud to be a 12%-er and associated with the most professional recruiting firm available."*

— Elaine Rudolphi
Team Leader
General Mills, Inc.

*"**PCS** is loaded with wisdom and gives the JMO interested in moving into a business career a leg up on the competition. Don't try a PCS to the business world without **PCS to Corporate America**. Roger offers valuable insight for every step of the way!"*

  — Doug Porter
   Executive Vice President
   Worldwide Management Director - McDonald's
   Leo Burnett Advertising

*"Five years after embarking on a career in Corporate America, **PCS** retains a prominent place on my business bookshelf. It is concise, loaded with guidance and insight, and continues to serve as a reminder of the reasons Corporate America comes to Roger to hire military officers—the ability to produce results in very demanding conditions. I strongly encourage embracing the wisdom and applying the principles in **PCS** not only during your transition but also throughout your career."*

  — Dave Burke
   Director, Telecommunications Group Systems
   Bell Atlantic

*"Read **PCS to Corporate America** as your first step in considering a transition from the military. Roger covers all aspects of the rewarding process of getting to know yourself and preparing yourself for a challenging civilian career. Roger understands the valuable assets you've developed as a JMO and tells you how to (and, perhaps, more importantly, how not to) demonstrate these skills during an interview. If you follow Roger's advice, you are sure to improve yourself and your chances of finding the civilian career you desire."*

  — Eric Treschuk
   Assistant Marketing Manager
   General Mills, Inc.

*"This plain-language, no-holds-barred manual about achieving goals is hands-down the most valuable reading I have ever done. The immediate bonus was an improvement in my military performance, the long-term reward was achieving a career as a consultant at Arthur Andersen. Read this book now and take it to heart. No matter where your future takes you, **PCS to Corporate America** will help you succeed at it!"*

  — Scott LePage
   Senior Consultant, Computer Risk Management
   Arthur Andersen

*"I cannot imagine trying to transition to Corporate America without reading **PCS**! Roger's step-by-step process told me exactly what to expect every step of the way, giving me the competitive edge I needed in tough interviews. Roger knows what companies look for and tells you how to use your military background to secure the best job offers. The investment you make in this book will pay back tenfold!"*

> — Debra Crew
> Associate Brand Manager
> Kraft Foods

*"**PCS to Corporate America** is the only SOP for success. The principles in this book are as crucial and practical today as they were 30 seconds before my first interview two years ago."*

> — Nelson Santini
> Project Manager
> Varco International

"Roger's wisdom has and continues to serve me well as I grow professionally and recruit JMOs. From the tools Roger imparted during the job hunting process to the critical look at myself that Roger made me dig deep to understand—all have had a significant impact on my career. Roger is the best in the business and knows what it takes to be a success."

> — Troy Barring
> Vice President of IVUS
> Boston Scientific-SCIMED

*"**PCS** should be your first step in considering a transition to Corporate America because you have to think like a business person first! Listen to what Roger has to say. People in the military are not out to make a profit....there is no bottom line. At the forefront of every business decision is the bottom line. Corporate America appreciates all the awards a candidate has received, the great performance reviews, etc. etc. But what a recruiter is really thinking is, 'How can this person improve shareholder value for my corporation?' Read **PCS** and make the principles of **PCS** part of your life."*

> — Kevin Crane
> Operations and Control Consultant, Corporate Audit
> International Paper

PCS TO CORPORATE AMERICA

From Military Tactics To
Corporate Interviewing Strategy

ROGER CAMERON

Odenwald Press
Dallas

PCS TO CORPORATE AMERICA
From Military Tactics To Corporate Interviewing Strategy

Copyright © 1990 Roger Cameron
Second edition 1994
Third edition 2000

Cover design by Ellen Fountain/Fountain Graphics

Published by Odenwald Press, Dallas, Texas

Library of Congress Cataloging in Publication Data

Cameron, Roger, 1935-
    PCS to corporate america: from military tactics to
    corporate interviewing strategy /
Roger Cameron--3rd ed.
        p. cm.
    Includes index.
    ISBN 1-884363-18-0
1. Employment interviewing. 2. Retired military personnel–
Employment. I. Title.

HF5549.5.I6 C35 2000
650.14'024'355--dc21

                                                        00-027696

Printed in the United States of America

CONTENTS

ACKNOWLEDGMENTS

I want to give a warm thank-you to the members of the Cameron-Brooks team who have been "cornerstones" for the writing of my books. Each has traveled thousands of miles with me during their careers, offering quality insight and advice. It would have been impossible to experience all of my success without them.

A special thank-you to Julie Welch for working with me on this third edition of *PCS*.

To my friends, business associates, clients and Cameron-Brooks alumni who continually encourage and support me, a special thank-you and appreciation. I have had the best job in America, having the opportunity to interact with so many exceptional people.

Those of you who have written words of praise as readers of *PCS* deserve a special acknowledgment. It has been inspirational to hear from thousands whose lives have been and continue to be impacted positively as a result of this book. I cannot count the number of individuals who have told me they consistently refer to *PCS* for promotional interview preparation and furthering their career. These individuals espouse the long-term value of the many lessons taught in this book.

I am appreciative of the Cameron-Brooks alumni in Corporate America who are adamant about hiring JMOs for their openings and hiring them from Cameron-Brooks. At every one of our

Career Conferences, it gives me great satisfaction to hear of the successes of our alumni and to work with the many alumni who attend our Conferences in search of hiring talented JMOs.

And, finally, thank you to the business world for believing in the quality of our military officers. Many of our client companies have been hiring junior officers from us for over 30 years and have watched the JMO move up the corporate ladder to the very top.

How To Gain The Most From This Book!

Hopefully, you are reading *PCS* long before you make your transition. While it is valuable at all times, its value is enhanced the earlier in your military career you read it.

I often talk with officers who share with me the value that *PCS* added to their successful transitions and business careers. Without fail, each of these officers recounts a systematic approach to reading the book, along with specific points that enabled them to retain and apply what they learned. I want to share the following three steps with you to help you, too, gain the most from *PCS*.

First Take a long evening and read *PCS* cover-to-cover. Do not stop to do the recommended exercises. It is important to understand all the points the book covers and the significance given to different issues.

Second Slowly reread *PCS* with the following supplies in hand:
- Three highlighters of different colors
  Determine your own code for highlighting issues of different intensity of importance.
- Small post-it notes
  Write key points to flag pages and signal points of significance.
- Varied colored pens
  Mark it up! Write in the columns. Make special

remarks relative to your situation and development.

Third   Now read the book again, and practice all exercises using a tape recorder and notebook for additional reference. Evaluate each exercise. Listen to the tapes with study partners whose judgment and constructive feedback will be of benefit. Take advantage of all material in the book, including the information in the Appendix. Practice, Practice, Practice!

PCS will become one of the most important books in your library. As your career progresses and you interview for promotion, do not assume you will automatically recall your interviewing techniques. Reread *PCS*. As you gain the responsibility of interviewing and hiring for your company and are required to identify individuals and recommend them for hire, your credibility is on the line. Reread *PCS*. Utilize *PCS* long-term and make it your primary career resource.

Most importantly, never loan your copy of *PCS* to anyone. I promise you won't get it back. The value of your remarks and references represents an extensive amount of dedicated time, along with important development notes that will make a difference in your career.

Direct your friends who want to borrow your copy of *PCS* to our web site at **www.cameron-brooks.com** where they can place a secure order online. For telephone orders, our toll-free number is 1-800-222-9235 in the U.S. or from Germany, 0800-85-22670. We'll have *PCS* in their hands in just two business days via priority mail!

FOREWORD

In 1990 I wrote the first edition of *PCS to Corporate America*. Since then I have received very positive feedback from JMOs regarding the book's value in helping them prepare for corporate interviews and a transition to the business world. However, the interviewing world is very dynamic—a world in which better methods of identifying and selecting talented employees are constantly evolving. In 1994 I rewrote *PCS*, identifying changes that had occurred, clarifying points, and bringing up new issues. Again, I received positive feedback. In 2000 it again is necessary to communicate to you the changes that have occurred in the world of corporate recruiting. I have rewritten *PCS* for a third time with the goal to continue to bring our candidates and other military officers to the marketplace better prepared. I feel confident that this updated edition includes enhancements that will benefit both your interviewing and business career success. As always, you must take **action** to gain the full benefit of this book.

My intent for this book is to address the bottom line. You won't find any "fluff." I felt it best to write a book you could get into immediately, one that focuses on what you need to do to be successful in interviews and to make a successful transition to the business world. I am confident this book will help you do exactly that.

You won't find in this book what you, as a military officer, already do so well. Many things are so innate to you that I don't need to discuss them. Often after having gone through my interviewing workshops, military officers come away feeling as if they will never do anything right. I always point out that I only address the issues you have a tendency to miss or do incorrectly. Reading a book about things that are natural to you and that you already know how to do would be a waste of your time and mine. Some of the suggestions in *PCS* may challenge you. However, I feel strongly that I cannot allow minor issues to prevent you from being successful when I could have mentioned them. I am proud to be one of the originators of the process that transitions military officers successfully to the business world. My goal is to help you do just that.

Throughout this book I recommend ways of addressing specific questions. It is not my intent that you repeat the verbiage word for word. Instead, use the suggested ideas and develop your own answers. Be yourself. If you allow a company to hire you while you hide behind a facade, it won't work. Ultimately, the company will wonder why they hired you. Make sure a company hires you for who you are rather than what you might pretend to be during your interviews. If some of the concepts in this book are new to you and you agree with them, begin immediately to use them at work and in your life. In this way, by the time you begin interviewing, you will be giving credible information to the recruiter.

Psychologically speaking, you have three selves—you at your best, you at your average, and you at your worst. **In an interview situation, you must be at your best.** Companies expect you to interview at 100 percent. This is the only percentage that will get you hired. During the entire career search process, you must be at your best. It is critical that you understand this concept. Companies will never believe you are better than what their recruiters see or hear in the interview. **Your goal as you prepare for a career transition is to achieve this percentage and nothing less.**

How do you achieve "being at you best"? Preparation. Hard work. Recruiters have said to me, "Roger, if an individual won't work hard to accomplish one of their own objectives (a great career), why should I assume he or she will work hard to accomplish objectives that we give them?" I have to agree. Amazingly, some officers will come to the marketplace assuming success without preparation. This is like you telling me that you are having an annual inspection on Monday morning and that you started preparation for the inspection on Friday. Or, like going to war without having practiced combat maneuvers. You know what will happen. You will fail. You may say that you should be natural interviewees. That would be great, but it won't work. Every officer I interview tells me they want an outstanding career with high compensation but not every officer is willing to commit to world-class preparation to accomplish this goal. You have to prepare for tough objectives. And, as you know, the harder you prepare, the more successful you are.

You learned this in grade school: The harder you studied, the easier your exams were and the higher your grade point average became. Everything in life is based on preparation. Not one of us is natural at everything we do.

I put our success for facilitating transitions to Corporate America against any other recruiting firm or recruiter in America. I have listened to what great companies are looking for, and I have seen the kind of individuals they are hiring to lead their companies into the future. I have seen the individuals who have gone to the top of Corporate America. I recognize the pattern. It is a pattern created from day one—the pattern of preparation and diligence—of people who do their work thoroughly. It is gratifying to watch the career progression of those officers I help transition to the business world.

Basically, there are three ways for the JMO to transition from the military to the business world:

1. Step **DOWN** into a business career. In this case the JMO takes a position that has less responsibility and less career potential than he or she had in the military. The JMO usually interviews for and accepts a position designed for the fresh college graduate. Companies who have less of an understanding of the capabilities of the JMO will try to hire you for a position like this.

2. Step **ACROSS** into a business career. In this case the JMO takes a position with responsibility and career opportunity that is equivalent to what he or she had in the military. The JMO interviews for and accepts a position that any JMO can fill. In other words, the company places value on the JMO's military experience (unlike the first situation) but does not distinguish between different caliber JMOs. While this type of career will utilize your skills, very rarely will it be a development position.

3. Step **UP** into a business career. In this case the JMO takes a development position with enhanced responsibility and career opportunity. The JMO interviews and accepts a position designed for a top caliber JMO. These are extremely competitive interviews in which the company looks for the best of the best. While these types of positions are highly desirable, they also require the highest level of preparation and skill development.

Cameron-Brooks only recruits for development positions in Corporate America. We work with officers who have a strong desire to step "up" into a business career. Early in the process candidates build their resumes, read business books, increase their skill package, and start working on how to handle the difficult interviewing questions. It seems the better the candidates are, the earlier they start their preparation. They are not procrastinators. They know it takes a lot of time and preparation to be at their best and to transition "up."

I am frequently asked, "What is the bottom line, Roger? What is Corporate America looking for in Development Candidates?" This is a good question, and there is an easy answer. They are looking for individuals who can get things done in spite of the difficulties that arise—**make-it-happen, goal-oriented, mission-oriented types. Leaders. Individuals who have a history of accomplishments. Basically, all-around high achievers.**

Corporations want people who do the following:

* Control their environment;
* Use their time effectively;
* Are extremely well-organized; and
* Know exactly what needs to be done, when it needs to be done and how to get it done.

Over the years, I have accepted only 12 percent of all the officers I have interviewed. Often, they say, "Roger Cameron is tough." I am tough because Corporate America is very demanding. Companies come to us to hire their future leaders. They only want to see the best of the best. I listen to my client companies. I bring them what they tell me they want.

Some people who are probably very good performers are not going to be hired because of their inability to communicate. What is more important than the ability to communicate, to persuade, to get your peers, superiors, team members, customers, and competition to see your point of view? People say, "Roger, if they would hire me, they would see that I'm a good performer." Sometimes,

I feel the same way. If they would just hire some military officers, they would discover how talented they are. Unfortunately, recruiting just doesn't work that way.

I encourage you to read this book with a positive attitude. Say to yourself, "I'm going to listen to an individual who has worked with military officers and helped transition them successfully to the business world for over three decades."

This book is written in a very direct way, but that is pretty much the way Corporate America thinks. I have watched recruiters decline individuals I felt were very capable. In fact, I knew they were good because I had read their performance evaluations, but, because they did not have the ability to communicate their successes, recruiters walked away from them.

People have often asked how I could stay in this business for over 30 years. I always give the same answer. In all these years, I have had thousands of jobs presented to me, yet I have never seen a job that interested me enough to take more than a casual look at it. I'm not so sure that there is a more exciting business than that of recruiting talented young men and women for top development positions with some of the best companies in Corporate America. It has been exciting to watch these young men and women move up the corporate ladder, have their successes, and become key leaders within their companies. I have received thousands of letters of appreciation over the years, and every one of them made me feel good. They made me realize how lucky I am to be in this business.

Officers we assisted—10, 15, 20 years ago—are still using many of the techniques our team and I taught them. I am very proud of our alumni. Each time I recruit an individual for Corporate America, I ask myself the question, "Do I want to put my name beside this individual as he or she transitions to the business world?" This is important to every member of the Cameron-Brooks team. We want to be proud of every candidate we help transition to the business world. And, of the overwhelming majority, we can be. We have had very few failures over the years.

This book will help you interview for any position in any organization. I would like to put my plug in for the profit-oriented world, the world of capitalism. It is a world that is exciting and challenging. When I think of how young America is, I realize that our greatness is based on the innovative nature of the United States. We have been leaders in numerous areas for many years. Sure, it is true that some countries have copied products we originated and made them better because of circumstances in their countries such as cheaper labor. But, I will still put America against anyone else. I will put our leaders, engineers, finance people, and information technology experts up against any in the world.

Working with the quality of companies I have represented over the years is very exciting. I have companies today who have a 20 to 40 percent annual growth factor and some of them even higher. When you take a highly sophisticated company that has this kind of growth, you need to have outstanding people to accomplish and manage it. The military officers I have introduced to the business world have loved the fact that they are not practicing but are, in fact, **doing**. What they learn on a daily basis, they can apply. When they go home at night, they can measure the fact that their company has been able to take a step closer to its objective. It is challenging but also satisfying to be in an environment in which you know you must constantly be changing and improving. It is also gratifying to work with positive-minded people who come to work in the morning because they **want** to be there, who are excited about what their company does and what their products can do for mankind, who find it exciting to be paid and promoted based on performance.

Recruiting military officers for Corporate America has always been interesting. I cannot say it has always been fun. I remember when I helped originate this business; I talked to companies about why they should hire military officers. I also remember some of their comments: "Excuse me, Roger, you're suggesting that we should hire somebody who operates in the world of nonprofit, in the world of appropriation instead of the world of profitability? Roger, what are we supposed to do with this individual who, for the last five years, has been involved with tanks, guns and artillery, airplanes and ships? I'm a little confused as to why we should hire this person. We should hire someone who is proud that he or she spends the entire budget? As a matter of fact, they even put it on their resumes."

That's the way things were when the military recruiting industry started. Interestingly, it has grown over the years—grown to the point where today military officers have demonstrated their value to Corporate America. Today, we can point to military officers who are presidents and CEOs of some of the top companies in Corporate America. Suddenly, corporate recruiters who have been cynics over the years about military officers are starting to take a very hard look at them. Today, companies are calling us rather than us calling them.

You've been good. As a matter of fact, you've been great! I don't know of any individual who has had more impact on Corporate America than the military officer. We admit to you that we made a lot of mistakes over the years in evaluating military personnel, but today we know you very well. We know what makes you successful and what your weaknesses are as you leave the military. We have developed programs that will bring you up to speed quickly in areas where you need more development. We know where to recruit to find a particular background. We know what you need to do in the military to make yourself successful in business. Today, we know the kind of private lifestyle you need for success in your business career. You were an unknown when we started this business. It has been fun to watch the progress of our candidates and yet agonizing to observe some of their failures. Fortunately, these failures are at a minimum in relation to what they were when we first started recruiting military officers.

After officers I have helped transition to Corporate America have been in the business world for a while, I often ask them what, if anything, they feel they have gained or lost by transitioning to the business world. Usually, I receive three positive answers and, in the old days, one negative answer.

The three positives I hear have never changed. The first positive is the quality of life—the ability to tell your sons or daughters with confidence that you are going to be at Little League at 6:00 P.M., to tell your family you'll be home for dinner, to know that evenings and weekends are yours, to set a vacation six months down the road and know that you will be there. I have rarely seen a vacation canceled by a company in all the years I've been associated with Corporate America.

The second positive relates to the input and control you have over your career. Companies ask you: "What is it you want to do? What kind of positions will enhance your career? What do you expect your company to do to ensure that you have a successful career?" You have a lot of input—veto rights for locations, positions, and the timing of promotions. When this veto right is exercised, it will RARELY have a negative influence on your career.

Third, our candidates have told us that their net worth has significantly increased. Why? Because companies provide exceptional retirement plans such as 401Ks, company-matching, and other savings vehicles, which allow employees at all levels to amass a significant amount of wealth. It used to be that most people in America created the bulk of their net worth through the equity built up in their homes, but two years ago we saw for the first time more equity in retirement plans than in one's home.

We get many other positive comments, but these three comments are the most significant in encouraging officers to make a career transition to the business world. The one negative we heard years ago is that officers felt they did not immediately enjoy the same degree of camaraderie in corporate life that they enjoyed in the military. We received this comment from military officers and their spouses. Today, when military officers join a company, usually former officers are there to greet them, and many companies now provide sponsors who will introduce you to the neighborhood and community. For the officer today, the transition to corporate life is easy and comfortable.

The Cameron-Brooks Alumni Association, made up of thousands of our candidates who have successfully transitioned to business, is a powerful influence in making the transition easier for our candidates. It is virtually impossible for you to come to Corporate America without being touched by Cameron-Brooks either by being hired, mentored, or managed by one of our alumni. This alumni network offers tremendous support to newly transitioned officers, their spouses (or significant others) and families. Our alumni will go out of their way to help make the transition as smooth as possible for you. One of the major reasons we have become such a powerful force in our industry is our alumni. Cameron-Brooks alumni are adamant about hiring junior officers for their positions and about hiring them from Cameron-Brooks.

As I've always said to military officers, it's not that one environment is good and the other bad. They are different. Some of you will determine that the military is better for you than the business world. We understand that. We like to think that as some of you read this book you will feel more confident that Corporate America is where you want to have your career. For those of you who make this choice, here's a word of caution. Do not think that Corporate America is going to be a cure-all for the problems you might have had in the military. We have our problems. Some of the things we do are not always smart. We are influenced by economic conditions, just as the military is.

There is no ideal company, job, or environment. However, I feel it is critically important that you come to Corporate America as an individual who intends to go to work for a great company and to stay with that company. I am a strong advocate of conducting thorough and proper analysis to determine which company is right for you. I do not encourage moving constantly from one company to another. Sometime during the course of your career, some personal challenges will arise that will divert you from your job. These challenges will cause you to need special focus on your family. You want to know that your company will support you during these difficult times. Too many times people switch from one company to another, looking for that better situation, only to find greater difficulties. If you expect the company to remain with you during the difficult times of your life, it is only fair that you stay with the company during difficulties they might have. Many employees want to leave a company when they see the product lose market share. They reason that it is okay for the company to support them during **their** difficult times, but they don't want to reciprocate when the **company** has difficult times. That is not fair. I encourage you to be loyal. Switching from one company to another will not always advance your career. All you have really done is change the problems. Every time you make a move, it is difficult for you and your family emotionally, and it tells many things about you that you may not want said.

I hope you find this book a valuable tool for preparing for corporate interviews and a career transition. Any time you have a question on an issue discussed in the book, feel free to contact me. I wish a book could cover everything, but I know it can't. It's similar to the preparation prior to our Career Conferences. We try to prepare for every question we think a candidate may encounter in an interview, but, after years of experience, I have found corporate recruiters can still surprise me. I think you will find the major issues for military officers are covered in this book. Have fun reading it, and the best of luck to you in your career search.

**STOP! STOP! STOP!
DON'T READ ANY MORE
OF THIS BOOK WITHOUT
A HIGHLIGHTER.**

Use a highlighter to emphasize those issues that are important to you. As a matter of fact, all of your interviewing and career transition preparation should be done with a highlighter and note pad in hand! Don't hesitate to write notes to yourself in the borders of each page so that you can quickly refresh your memory and flip back through the book.

PCS is a career reference book. It is a book I hope you will read, refer to, reread, and refer to again as your career progresses. Do not loan it or any other reference book from your personal library. Throughout your career these books should never be out of arm's reach. There are some books I reread every year to remind me of valuable points. Every quality book should be read, referred to, and reread.

=CHAPTER 1=

The Evaluation Process

*"Roger is the recognized authority in his industry. His 30-plus years of experience give him a unique perspective of candidates and Corporate America. Roger is demanding, doesn't mince words and consistently challenges you. No one works harder to give you that little edge. Listen to him–he will make you better. Within five years of transitioning from the military I was serving on the senior leadership team of a $3 billion company with 20,000 associates. Roger has impacted my life and the way that I think about success more than any other teacher, coach, or mentor. Reading **PCS** will ensure that you are well prepared to rise to the occasion and seize the opportunities."*

      — Tim Fliss
        Vice President, Human Resources
        Schneider National

CHAPTER 1 ════════════════════════

The Evaluation Process

Early Recruiting Days

Corporate America initially believed that the military officer would have a difficult time being competitive in the business world as a Development Candidate. There were three basic reasons for this belief.

When we first started recruiting the military officer, most were leaving the military five to seven years after their age group graduated from college and entered the business world. That meant officers spent five to seven years in the nonprofit world (the military) and were then entering the world of profitability. Given the difference in experiences, how could the military officer logically catch up to his or her business world contemporaries in minimum time?

I compare this situation to a track race in which you are competing with recent college graduates. To be considered a winner, you have to finish in the top 10 percent. No problem, you say. But, when you get to the track and you're in the blocks, I reach down to tap you (the military officer) on the shoulder and I say, "By the way, when I pull the trigger, you stay at the blocks. Wait until all the college graduates in your age group get a fifth of the way around the track. Then you may start." Undoubtedly, you would stand up and say, "Come on, Roger, that's not realistic." Similarly, it makes sense that you, the military officer, would have a hard time catching up with your age group as you entered the business world. You notice that I said **age** group, not **year** group.

In the military, you need to be concerned about being competitive with your **year** group. In contrast, when you begin a career in business, you are measured by your **age** group.

As we examined the bulk of officers coming out of the military, we discovered that well over 90 percent of you had never used your education as it was designed to be used. Education is a tool in the business world, not a ticket. This was a second strike against you.

The third reason companies believed military officers were going to have difficulty being competitive in the business world was that we had a difficult time making a connection between many of your positions in the military and what we had to offer in Corporate America. What could a Damage Control Assistant, Field Artillery Officer, Infantryman or an Intelligence Officer do in the business world? We knew there existed some relatable knowledge, but we were not sure it was enough to overcome the disadvantage of time.

Post-Vietnam Recruiting
What forced recruiters to rethink this situation? The Vietnam War! Corporate recruiters discovered that when they went to the college campus to hire Development Candidates, there weren't enough students available due to the draft. Suddenly, recruiters had to reassess the military officer as a potential hire. Corporations started hiring officers, but reluctantly, because they felt officers would have a hard time competing with their age group. Because of this, officers interviewed for only a small fraction of the positions they see today. But, as Corporate America measured your performance in the business world against the very best from the college campus, they discovered you were catching up very quickly.

This was an exciting discovery for the corporate world. All of a sudden, companies had two supply sources for hiring Development Candidates—the college campus and the military. In most cases, companies were hiring more college students than military officers, sometimes by a ratio of 80/20. However, many companies today have virtually reversed this ratio as they have witnessed military officers effectively transfer their military skills to the business world and immediately make an impact.

Over the years, interest, enthusiasm, and excitement for the military officer have grown. Today, I can point my finger to officers who have made the transition, have been highly successful, and have made their way to the top of major corporations. Today, more and more companies are eager to hire military officers and benefit from your ability to make things happen and make them happen better. Companies specifically seek out military officers to fill unique leadership roles with more responsibility, more opportunity for upward mobility, and in a wider range of job positions and career fields than ever before.

The Development Candidate

Not all career paths are the same in the business world. Industry to industry and company to company, there are differences in the way a company will structure a career path. Fundamentally, there are two types of career paths—development and non-development.

The **Development** career is designed for candidates who will be future leaders in a company. While you will always fill specific jobs as a Development Candidate, the company will expose you to various functions within a corporation to develop you as a generalist. Regardless of where you start your development career, as your career progresses, the company will teach you skills in finance, accounting, information technology, supply chain management, operations, sales, marketing, human resources, etc. The intent of such broad knowledge is to develop your skills to be a future leader in the company. Without these general management skills, a person cannot lead a company (just as a general or admiral cannot lead in the military without excellent combined forces knowledge).

A Development Candidate needs to have a burning desire to rise to the top 10 percent of major corporations and the perceived ability to accomplish that objective. It is important that you understand (as you enter the business world) how you, as a commissioned officer, fit into a major corporation. Corporate America will spend a lot of time, money, expertise, and effort getting you (the Development Candidate) to the point where you can have a major impact on the direction of your company.

A **Non-Development** career seeks people to fill jobs in a specific area of expertise. These managers are not targeted to be the future top 10 percent leaders of a company but rather are oriented toward developing an expertise in one functional area of a company. It's not that they can't be Development Candidates but rather that their goal is to develop along the line of a specialist. Regardless of where you start your career as a Non-Development Candidate, your career path is designed to make you a future expert in one area of the company (engineering, IT, finance, HR, etc.). As an example, let's say you begin your career in Information Technology. As your career progresses, you will learn more and more about a company's IT infrastructure, perhaps specializing in security, broadband networks, or enterprise databases. These positions are important in any company because experts ensure that a company can get maximum return on capital, but the key is that experts never lead companies.

I am not saying that one career path is more important than the other, but they are radically different. As you consider your options in the business world, it is important that you determine the type of career in which you are interested. Remember, not all companies hire Development Candidates. Some companies and industries have no programs in place to develop future leaders and thus have no interest in recruiting Development Candidates. These industries and companies "pool" promote, which means all hires jump into the pool and whoever floats to the top when a management spot becomes available gets promoted. Most new companies start out this way as they do not have the depth of personnel to develop leaders from within the company. However, as many companies mature and become more sophisticated, they will move toward the hiring of Development Candidates (fast trackers) as a means of developing future leaders from within the company.

Career progression in a company is not an overnight venture any more than it is in the military. Advancing from LTJG through LT to LCDR and up the chain of command takes time and a considerable amount of investment. There are many things you need to learn and experiences you must have to become a top-level leader in a company. It is important to realize that these steps are necessary, and it takes time for them to happen. No matter what the size of the company or the type of business, there are few "overnight sensations" in Corporate America.

The business world wants Development Candidates who are "growable" people. This is what having that "burning desire" to be a top 10 percent leader is all about. In other words, **you understand the investment that it takes to be a leader in a successful organization.** Hoping or simply wanting success is worthless without the burning desire to prepare for it.

Over the last 30 years, I have interviewed literally tens of thousands of JMOs. So many of them will say they want to be successful, but, unfortunately, a small percentage know the investment in personal growth that it is going to take to get there. Find any group of the top 10 percent of leaders in the business world, and I promise you will find people who are constantly reading and expanding their knowledge base and skill set. These individuals know the importance of a diverse skill base, and they work on becoming knowledgeable in all areas of a company, not just their specific position or function. They seek higher degrees as they advance in age, keeping their formal education current so they remain competitive and in position for promotion. They know there is no substitute for knowledge, so they are constantly in the learning mode. They have outstanding leadership ability and interpersonal skills. They are mission-oriented leaders with a track record of making significant contributions to their past organizations. This is what I mean when I talk about having a burning desire to be in the top 10 percent of the leadership of a company.

Should You Use A Recruiting Firm?
Anyone reading this will feel this is a biased, opinionated statement. To a degree, it is. Nevertheless, the answer is "yes." Without fail the first thing you should do once you have made the decision to enter the business world is to become associated with a quality recruiting firm.

Most companies prefer to hire through recruiting firms. If their normal ratio for hiring is one out of 200 interviews, a company is going to be very reluctant to turn down 199 people who are going to be out on the street as potential buyers of their product. Rejected job applicants may buy a competitor's product just because the other company turned them down. For the company, it's much less "costly" to have a recruiting firm say "no" to the majority of applicants.

Quality recruiting firms are evaluated by the success the client company has in terms of the number and quality of talent they hire. The measuring tool companies use to judge recruiting firms is based on the factor of 10 interviews. When a company seeks the help of a recruiting firm to fill their openings and interviews 10 people, on the average how many do they say "yes" to? Of every 10 people they pursue beyond the first interview, how many receive offers? For every 10 who are offered jobs, how many accept? And, for every 10 who accept, how many are successful and promotable? Companies judge recruiting firms very carefully. It will be important for you (in making your decision) to determine the recruiting company with whom it will be best for you to partner (depending on your needs, interests, situation, openness to location, etc.). In making your choice, I encourage you to use a recruiting firm that has developed outstanding relationships with its client companies.

Many of you come to us suggesting that two or three recruiting firms represent you. We understand your reasoning. It's just that recruiting firms that work with candidates over an extended period of time and prepare them for corporate interviews put in a tremendous amount of time and effort on your behalf. This is a large investment on their part. Obviously, these recruiting firms are not willing to develop individuals so they can interview on their own or through another recruiting firm. If you're going to choose one of the best recruiting firms, it is to your advantage to be loyal to that company until they have had the chance to show you to their client companies. I know of no recruiting firm in America that asks for 100 percent exclusivity. If they do, walk away from them. However, for a **quality** recruiting firm to ask for exclusivity **until after** they have shown you to their client companies is simply good business.

Can you do a search on your own? Yes, absolutely. Usually, it is much more costly, but it can be done and done successfully.

Networking with associates in various organizations and handing your resume to someone you know who works for a company and who in turn can hand it to a hiring manager on your behalf are the best ways to conduct a search on your own. Your success is limited when you send your resume to companies without knowing people there who can recommend you to the hiring manager. Many companies have thousands of candidates applying on a weekly basis, so putting a resume into that mass and hoping a company will call you is going against all odds. Having a friend, acquaintance, or parent hand your resume to a hiring manager of their company can ensure better success than the mail-in route.

If you are an officer doing your own search, it will be difficult for you to verify that a position is a development position. I'm not sure how you would do this. If you ask, and I would, you would probably want further verification.

Other disadvantages to conducting a search on your own are that 1) it is difficult to explore as diverse opportunities as a recruiting firm will show you, and 2) as you interview with companies individually and receive offers individually, you will only be able to evaluate one offer at a time. Most companies won't allow you to keep an offer for a long period. A good recruiting firm can show you several opportunities at one time. Also, quality recruiting firms will work closely with you during the "follow-up process" (the weeks that follow an initial interview in which companies invite candidates for second and third interviews and extend offers to those candidates who best fit their criteria and culture). During the follow-up process, quality recruiting firms will help you evaluate your different offers and arrive at the career decision that is best for you.

Today, you can post your resume on the Web. However, most of these positions are for Non-Development Candidates or for those who already have specific business experience. As good as it might seem, companies have responded more negatively than positively about this new avenue for job seekers. They say they are fed up with the tens of thousands of resumes they receive on a weekly basis via the Web. Resumes received online seem to clog up the system with applicants whose qualifications are incompatible with the company's needs. I have seen few officers have any luck in finding high potential development positions through an Internet search.

The Internet is a great information source. I encourage you to use it actively to research companies, positions, and the business world in general. The Web is not a perfect information distribution system, but it is a direct pipeline to information. Company web sites offer information similar to what you might see in company literature or brochures. Studying individual company web sites is a great start for learning about different industries and companies.

Some officers will not earn the right to be represented by a recruiting firm. That's not a harsh statement—it's an honest statement. Every recruiting firm which agrees to represent an officer must ask themselves, "Does my client company need to pay me a fee to find this person?" Unfortunately, many times that answer is "no." We are not suggesting that the person is not a quality person and a potential good hire for a company, but client companies are very specific about the skill set of individuals they want us to recruit for them.

At our recruiting firm, we have said over the years, "We have the knowledge and capability to show candidates as many high-potential positions in the business world for which they are qualified. We know how to guide candidates through a successful transition, and we know how to develop candidates so their start in the business world is on a track for moving up." Candidly speaking, we want to get reimbursed for that time, effort, and knowledge. It's just good business.

Present a quality picture of yourself to your recruiting firm. Officers sometimes make statements that cause me to rule them out. They will rationalize, "Well, I wouldn't say that to a company." Let me emphasize, "You have just said it to a company." You must remember that a recruiting firm is retained by the corporation. If you make the statement to us, it's like making it to the company. We can't ask you not to make a statement. We can't be unprofessional and suggest you cover up what you said, or say, "Don't dare say that in front of the company; they won't hire you."

Officers have told me they're not sure whether they want to go into the business world. That's fine, the business world is not for everyone. But, can you imagine a company saying, "Roger, we want to pay you a fee to find us an individual who's not certain whether they want to operate in the profit-oriented or the non-profit world." These are diametrically opposed operating philosophies. We can only agree to partner with you as you transition if you are someone who has a **burning desire** to enter the profit-oriented world, be a capitalist, and rise to the top. We must **hear** that desire.

Some individuals say to me, "Several years down the road, I want to have my own business." I have to rule those individuals out. You wouldn't want someone to walk into your place of business and say, "I want you to develop me, educate me, increase my skill package, and pay me a high salary. Then, I can become an expert, save money, go across the street, open my own business, and go into competition against you."

I'm not asking you to be dishonest. I am asking you to evaluate what you want to do with your professional career. If it is to open your own business, I respect that. After all, I own my business. But don't use somebody else to do it. Just go open your business and be successful. If you want a career in Corporate America, then come committed. Use all of the development opportunities my client companies will offer. Be a leader within that company. Go to the top. Things can change in the future, but to start a high-potential development career with a company knowing you're going to leave them in the near future is purely unprofessional and dishonest.

Give the recruiting firm the information they need to professionally represent you. Produce quality applications and supporting file material. Never refer to your resume on your application. I interview more than 20 people a day. I don't have time to review over 20 different resume formats to find the information you're referencing. Take time to fill out your application and other forms thoroughly, carefully, and accurately. Show us you believe your application material is important. You want to be represented as the professional person we know you are. Don't wait until the last minute to get your college transcripts. Get everything ahead of time. Document everything sent to your recruiting firm, and keep a copy yourself. Watch your spelling and sentence structure. Keep the material in your file current as your job title or other information changes. As you get new officer evaluations, forward them to your recruiting firm. Your career transition is too important for you not to be extremely organized, timely, thorough, and willing to work with the recruiting firm regarding the material in your file so they can best represent you to their client companies.

SLOPPY APPLICATION MATERIAL = DECLINE

Many applications cause us to decline the officers immediately. I say to myself, "I don't even want to take the time to write a decline letter, put a stamp on it, and mail it." This file doesn't warrant taking our time, but, professionally, we do it anyway. As sloppy application material is sent to us, we say to ourselves, "Obviously, this wasn't very important to the candidate because it is so sloppy." These applications could misrepresent you—on the other hand, they may not!

You want to work with a quality recruiting firm. Check out the firm. Ask to speak with former candidates with whom they partnered and successfully transitioned to business. Ask the recruiting company about their program and success rate. How do they prepare candidates for a transition? What percentage of the candidates are successful at a conference? You have every right to know this information. It's important for you to get a recruiting firm that works in partnership with you. Unfortunately, some recruiting firms only send your resume to different companies and hope the companies respond. Unless a recruiting firm is doing a lot for the company—screening your background thoroughly and working with you to educate you about business and to build your skill package, it is doubtful the recruiting firm represents much value to a company. The great companies in Corporate America are smart. They put their money where they get the best value.

I've heard officers say, "I've already been accepted by another recruiting firm." I say, "When were you interviewed?" They answer, "I haven't been interviewed. I was accepted over the phone." What would Procter & Gamble, Dell Computer Corporation, Arthur Andersen, Johnson & Johnson, or any other quality company say if a recruiting firm calls them to say, "We want you to interview a candidate we haven't seen." Can you imagine that? If a recruiting firm isn't willing to commit the time and expense to come to your base or post, interview you, and work with you over a period of time, do you really need them?

Many of you tell me that recruiting firms don't want to talk to you unless you're within three to six months of getting out of the military. Do you realize what that recruiting firm is saying? They don't want to do the work it takes to develop you and set you up for success in the business world. They don't want to look into your background and help you do what you need to do to transition "up." They don't want to invest time and effort into developing officers; they simply want to place you with a company. They're saying, "No, we just want to show you to a company, hope you get placed, and receive our fee."

Make sure the recruiting firm is willing to do the kind of work it will take to develop you over a period of time. You don't need a recruiting firm that looks at you with a dollar figure in mind. Unfortunately, too many recruiting firms do just that. When you know major companies are paying top dollar to recruiting firms to select, interview, develop, and bring talented people to them, you have every right to demand certain standards. It is your professional future you are placing in the hands of a recruiting firm, and you owe it to yourself to work with a recruiting firm that is going to give you the best possible start and future in a business career.

The Evaluation Process
Last year in my travels around the world looking for Development Candidates for our client companies, I interviewed over two thousand officers from the Navy, Air Force, Army, and Marine Corps. Out of the two thousand, I was able to accept only 12 percent. This was not by design but by normal evaluation of credentials and what was stated in the interview against the needs and requirements of our corporate clients. What makes me consistently able to accept **only** 12 percent of the officers I interview? Let's look at the evaluation process.

Three Categories Of Your Life
If you were to look at the profiles of the top 10 percent of

management in business today, you would find certain common-alties (behavioral traits, attributes, skills) that go all the way back to high school. If you come to an interview talking only about what you have done in the military, you're attempting to stand on only one of three legs—the other two being your high school and college careers.

We evaluate **equally** the performance factors in your high school, college, and military careers. Equally is the key word. First, we evaluate high school records on quantifiable factors: the grade point average, the size of your class, your ranking within that class and SAT/ACT scores. This gives us a good indication of how you compared to the performance of other students. We look at the difficulty of the curriculum. Was it an honors program? Did you challenge yourself all four years of high school? Then, we look at extracurricular activities. What did you do outside of academics? In extracurricular activities, our most important questions are: "Were you elected to leadership roles by your peers or superiors?" and "What contribution did you make?" We would also like to see the beginning of a positive work ethic. Overall, we look to see how motivated you were to do more than only what was required of you.

After looking at your high school accomplishments, we evaluate your college years. We cover the same areas and questions used in evaluating high school performance, but we add two critical factors—the known quality of your college or university and the known quality of your curriculum.

What is the first thing we look for in the military? The positions you've held. In your particular branch were these positions career enhancing? Did you get them at the right time? Did you hold them for the right length of time? We then proceed to your officer evaluations. We look for impact statements—statements that indicate high achievement and set you apart from your peers.

Each of you knows (in the different branches of the military) the evaluation inflation factor. So do we. We know every nuance, every idiosyncrasy of individual statements made in your officer evaluations. We also look at your academic performance. Remember Corporate America is an academic environment. Therefore, your performance in military schools is important.

Then, we look at more subjective factors. This is the conversational portion of the interview. We evaluate the following:

1) Your ability to develop instant rapport;
2) Your use of first names;
3) Your body language; and
4) Your ability to communicate persuasively.

We start with poise, self-confidence, and interpersonal skill. This is important because you will be placed in a new environment and be expected to make an immediate impact. You must have the poise, confidence, and people skills to move into an unknown situation and perform quickly. You need to be able to get buy-in from people across the organization (your team members, peers, and superiors) and have the ability to create a positive work environment.

You must be able to communicate persuasively in order to make an impact in as short a period of time as possible. Show us you use time effectively. There are many ways to make that determination even though, for the most part, it is a subjective evaluation.

Finally, we look for a person who is constantly striving to grow. Sometimes, when we evaluate an officer's high school and college experiences, we find extremely outstanding credentials. We ask ourselves, "How did they get it all done?" However, when we get to the military, we discover they do **nothing** but their job. We don't see the growth outside the job. The military encourages you to design your life around your job. We're not saying the military is wrong in that. We're simply saying that's not what we're looking for in Corporate America. We seek individuals who have continued to develop their family interest, extracurricular activities, and life outside the military. We want to see continued academic growth. We have little interest in a person whose age has advanced but whose formal education has not.

We look for people who have developed outside interests, and we don't really care what they are. We like to see a good balance between intellectual and activity-oriented interests, but we don't care whether it's running, hiking, handball, family outings, reading, computers, writing, chess, flying, boating, camping, Boy Scouts, Girl Scouts, Young Life or Big Brothers/Big Sisters. We like to see a diversity of activities. We're not looking for carbon copies. We want to see people who are involved—people who are growing.

We are interested in your personal life, as well, so when you are discussing extracurricular activities, be honest with us. Tell us what you do. **Don't create an answer for us. Don't tell us what you think we want to hear.** Tell it the way it is. We want to know about all aspects of your life. Learn to be comfortable with yourself as an individual as well as with your ability to perform and make an impact.

Companies cannot mandate that their employees work well with others. At any time, employees can resign and walk out the door. Therefore, we look to hire people who are professional and have good interpersonal skill—people who are respected by others, who work well with others, and who are eager to come to work each morning. Companies want individuals who have the ability to create positive work environments. We're not interested in the cocky person whose self-confidence controls them. We want people who have total control of their self-confidence. They don't have to wear it on their sleeve. They know they're good. They don't have to act as if they're the best.

I have learned that the really good people do not inflate numbers. The confident officers are not afraid to tell me that on a scale of 1-10, they're an 8 in leadership ability, a 6 in computer and information technology skills, or a 5 in mechanical aptitude. Only those who lack self-confidence feel they must tell me they're a 10 in everything they do. We want people who have good self-insight—people who know themselves. They can honestly identify their strengths and weaknesses. They want a company to hire them for who they are not what they pretend to be in an interview.

Do we always get a perfect candidate? In all my years of recruiting, I probably never have. We take an individual's entire history of background material from high school through the military and put the positives on one scale and the negatives on the other scale. We do, however, want the positive side of the scale to crash to the floor. This is the type of talented individual who makes it to the top of Corporate America and whom we can get very excited about hiring.

Computer Literacy
We are in the middle of an Information Revolution. Every development role in the business world is being affected by the enabling role of information technology (IT). To be a Development Candidate, you will need strong IT skills (regardless of the type of career field in which you have an interest). IT is a driving force behind the growth in Corporate America, and all business **leaders** of the future must have a track record of applying IT to solve complex problems. It is difficult to overstate the profound effects of IT in Corporate America. Today, we can show 30-40

percent more positions to candidates with strong computer skills. I expect this percentage will only continue to grow.

Unfortunately, the military (some branches and functional areas more than others) is behind the business world regarding IT. As a result, it is likely that you will have to catch up to your peers who have been in business during the boom in IT. The upside is that you have a lot of resources today that you can use to improve your knowledge of IT.

If you are only a user of IT, develop a strategy to improve your skills today. The key is to develop enough knowledge to help you solve complex problems using IT as a tool. In other words, you have a process problem at work, and you use IT to improve work flow, reduce bottlenecks, and improve results. You have a data management problem, and you use IT to develop a new database to improve knowledge sharing, etc. This is what I mean by using IT to solve problems.

Learn On A PC At Work
The quickest way to improve your IT skills is to take on a project at work where you can learn a new technology and apply it to solve a problem. Most PCs in the military are Windows based and come with Microsoft Excel and Access. This is where you need to start.

Specifically:

*   Become familiar with Windows and/or Windows NT. At the very least, you should be an expert in Windows before you leave the military.

*   Take advanced level classes in both Excel and Access and start using them to improve processes. Just being an expert

at Microsoft PowerPoint will do you no good in a business career. Excel and Access are much more broadly used for statistical analysis, managing data, reporting, and process improvement. You can find good classes in Excel and Access through the military or civilian programs.

• Seek out references at a bookstore in these applications (there are literally thousands of books on each).

Improve Your Knowledge Of Computer Networks
While strong PC skills are invaluable, you also will benefit from learning the essentials of computer networks. Remember, all PCs in the business world are networked, and it will be difficult for you if you do not have at least a basic knowledge of NIC cards, hubs, routers, switches, cabling, and network protocols like TCP/IP and ETHERNET. I recommend you take a class at a local community college on the essentials of computer networks. There are literally thousands of certification programs where you can take classes on this subject. You can also buy books at a bookstore on the subject (try the Dummies series). Get involved in a network related project at work so you can get hands-on experience.

Learn How To Write Programs
Programming is not what it used to be. In the past only programmers had to know how to program a computer. Today, if you want to solve a tough problem, you will have to understand how software is developed, modified, tested, and implemented. I recommend you start with the Internet. Learn how to write HTML and JAVA so you can develop web sites for your unit. You can take classes in both. I also think Visual Basic is an excellent language to learn as you can use it to customize Access databases and Excel workbooks.

Some other good investments of your time: Microsoft Project, Oracle, SAP, ATM, UNIX, and C++.

Finally, remember only you can improve your knowledge and skills. No one can do it for you. Do not rely on what you learned four or five years ago in school. It is outdated. If you are not able to leave the military for several years, make sure you are getting good advice about how to keep up with cutting-edge technology. Develop a plan to improve your skills while you are in the military so you remain on par with your peers in the business world. You will dramatically improve the number of development opportunities with which you can interview upon leaving the military.

Immediate Impact
As you enter Corporate America, you are expected to perform immediately. Officers often say, "Roger, could you tell me how a company in the business world is going to train me?" I encourage you to be cautious in overstating the need to be trained.

Corporations **train** fresh college graduates. Corporations do not expect to spend a lot of dollars or time to train military officers. You received training in the military, and you bring that valuable training to Corporate America. There's no reason why you shouldn't be able to have an impact on profitability (the bottom line) instantly. You've learned how to accomplish difficult objectives. You've learned how to prioritize, organize, and effectively manage time, to break tough objectives down into component parts, and to motivate your team members and peers to help accomplish those objectives. Whether you're applying your expertise to solve a problem in the military world or a problem in the business world, the methods are the same. You need to suggest that as a military officer **you can make an immediate impact**. Companies will pay you more than a recent college graduate, and you will expect to be promoted faster than a recent college graduate because you already have had "training" that is valuable and costly. Most college graduates do not bring this to the table.

After all, if you're going to catch up with your age group, you'll want to get in and get started immediately. The less time you take to become effective, the more quickly you can move ahead of your age group into significant management roles.

Most companies provide you with some orientation to the new work environment, but orientation is different from training. Orientation is basically what is considered as "on the job training" in the military. At the same time you are performing, you also are learning.

So, rather than emphasize the need for training, show that you, the military officer, have the flexibility to adapt to the ever-changing, highly competitive corporate environment. You have the right attitude, and you will succeed in making an immediate impact in this environment. Give a recruiter proof and evidence of these qualities in your interviews.

Throughout this book I talk about characteristics or competencies, such as IT skills, being flexible, and having a positive attitude, that companies look for in Development Candidates. This does not mean you need to possess all or be strong in each of the characteristics I mention nor that every company looks for the same characteristics or competencies. Every candidate is unique, and every company and position is unique. I mention them to you to get you to think about the characteristics and competencies you possess and to know which ones are important to bring to light in an interview. As you read this book, refer to Appendix A for a list of key competencies recruiters look for in the Development Candidates they interview.

CHAPTER 2

The Crucial First Impression

*"**PCS to Corporate America** is the how-to manual for transitioning to the civilian world. It walks you step-by-step through the entire interview process. Starting with an evaluation of what you have to offer a company, you'll learn how to assemble a resume, how to prepare for the interview and, finally, how to present the best you during the interview. All of Roger's expertise in helping military officers get the careers they want is in this book."*

— Vivian Henderson
Senior Systems Analyst
Thomson Consumer Electronics

CHAPTER 2

The Crucial First Impression

What is the **first impression** you make to a prospective employer? In the hundreds of speeches I've given around the world, I've often asked my audiences this question. And, in the many years I've been in this business, I have rarely heard the answer I believe is the correct one.

People say it's the appearance you make as you step into the recruiter's office: your suit, your dress, your grooming, the sparkle in your eyes, your voice inflection, your walk, your handshake. I emphatically believe all these factors make up the second impression.

The first impression is your resume or application. In 99 percent of these cases, the resume is seen even before an application.

POOR RESUMES/
POOR APPLICATIONS =
DECLINE

Recruiters, believe it or not, are human beings. As they evaluate your resume, they form an impression. It can be one of tremendous interest—or of no interest at all. Unfortunately, many times when I look at resumes, they do little to interest me. Let's focus on what a resume should do for you.

RESUMES:
THE VITAL INFORMATION

Gathering Information

I always am amazed when individuals bring me half-finished applications because they did not anticipate needing to have certain information, such as transcripts, at their fingertips. Before you start the process of building your resume or filling out company applications, you should gather together all pertinent information. Create a file containing your high school and college transcripts, all of your academic and performance evaluations, past employment history, social security and driver's license numbers, etc.

Availability Date

First and foremost, a resume should tell a recruiter your date of availability. A position is open. The date you are available will need to coincide with that position being open or when the position will be open. You may be the best candidate going, but, if your availability doesn't coincide with the appropriate time for the company, then you're of no value to that company. Many corporate recruiters are confused regarding the military's exit process—understandably so. Don't let your availability date be a guessing game for the recruiter.

Level Of Education

Next, show your level of education. It's important because positions often call for a specific educational background. If your education isn't right for this particular position, the recruiter must move on to the next resume. I want to caution you to put accurate academic information on both your resume and any application(s) you are asked to complete. What your resume and application state must be identical to what is stated on your transcript(s). Frequently, officers will tell me their transcript is wrong. If there is an error on your transcript, get it corrected immediately and certainly before you begin a career search. I assure you this is considered a serious breach of accuracy, and you need to be on top of any such situations.

Accomplishments

When you list **significant accomplishments** (which is basically what resumes should do), remember that in Corporate America no accomplishment is considered significant unless it impacts the bottom line. Your ability to communicate your significant accomplishments both on your resume and in your interviews is most important. If you cannot describe past accomplishments, you will have a very difficult time having a successful career search.

Recently, for example, an officer asked me my opinion of his resume. "Are you sure you want me to comment?" I asked. He said, "Yes" (his curiosity aroused). I said, "I'm amazed you would build a resume that suggests you've been a failure."

Why, in fact, was there strong proof of failure in his resume? After all, his resume told what his responsibilities were. It gave his job title, dates of that position, and the duties assigned to him. He was a commander, had 120 subordinates, and was responsible for their combat readiness, health, and welfare. There were several lines of this information, and then he went on to his previous position. He wrote down his entire military career. But, here is the point—his resume failed to list his accomplishments. **It listed his responsibilities, but, remember, with any responsibility, you can fail or succeed.** You can fail to certain degrees. You can succeed to certain degrees. A recruiter could only assume he had no successes with his responsibilities. What we want to know on your resume, more than anything, is this: **When you were given a responsibility, what did you do with it? What were your accomplishments?** On your resume state the back end of a responsibility, rather than the front end. Recruiters are interested in results.

We also are interested in the bottom line. In your descriptions of your back end results, refer to the bottom line of the military—combat readiness. Every action you take, regardless of your position, should further this cause. Also keep in mind that the military wants you to achieve your objective at minimum cost. You need to be able to talk about your accomplishments in terms of the bottom line and the military's push for doing more with less, because this is exactly what a recruiter wants to believe you will have the ability to do for their company in the business world.

Stating Your Objective

Caution: Officers working with a recruiting firm should follow the firm's <u>specific</u> guidelines on objectives.

You must have an **objective** on your resume. Don't be vague or general in your objective. "Position in management, building upon an ability to balance multiple projects while still attaining overall goals by virtue of detailed planning and thoughtful delegation of responsibility." This tells most recruiters that you don't know exactly what you want to do. Furthermore, you have used the words "position in management." Most of the top companies in Corporate America develop management from within. Consequently, you have just eliminated yourself from many of the top companies in Corporate America. Be careful of the word "management" when, in fact, you mean "supervision."

Frequently, officers make the statement that they want to start in one of the following:
- A mid-level management position;
- A lower mid-level management position;
- An upper mid-level management position; or
- An entry-level management position.

In the many years I have been recruiting military officers, I have never facilitated a career transition directly into a management role. Our client companies simply do not hire management from outside. Imagine yourself working for a company for a four or five-year period. A management spot opens up above you, and then the company goes outside to hire someone for that position. You would be very unhappy. You would be demoralized, and that company would have a morale problem on its hands.

Frequently, the word "management" is misused. It is confused with the word "supervision." Here's how we succinctly articulate the difference between management and supervision. In the military, you're not a manager until you reach the level of colonel or above, because managers set big picture objectives. Supervisors motivate the members of their team to carry out the objectives that management establishes. We would suggest that a company commander is a supervisor carrying out the objectives that battalion or upper-level management, colonel or above, establishes for him or her. This is not to say that one is good or one is bad—it just clarifies where you are in the hierarchy of a company. So, if officers would use the word "supervisor" to indicate that they are looking for a supervisory position instead of a management position, they would find that their resumes would be read, and the odds for pursuit would increase.

Give an objective that is directed, such as "sales leading to management," "staff engineering," "management information systems," "line operations," "manufacturing," "operations," etc. Be specific. Tell a recruiter you are a person who knows what you want to do. **Demonstrate that you have done a thorough analysis, studied the business world, and have a good feeling for where you will fit best.** When you leave the military as an officer, you are behind your age group who went straight from college into business. Therefore, in order to catch up, you must have conviction plus a definite career objective.

It is better to build two, three, or even four different resumes, based on different objectives, than to have one resume with an objective that attempts to cover everything.

Supporting The Primary Objective

One of the most critical points in a resume is that your accomplishments must support the primary objective of the position you held.

Let's consider the commander with 120 subordinates. What do we want to know more than anything else? We want to know that his or her troops are ready for combat. That's most important. Once a company commander told me his best accomplishment was that his mess hall was voted best mess of the quarter, three quarters in a row. But, the mess hall is a collateral responsibility, not a primary one. If this had been stated after several primary accomplishments, it would have been better received.

If you expect to be a successful supervisor in Corporate America, then you should highlight (in your accomplishments) what you did with your supervisory experience. Tell about your successes in motivating members of your team. Understand that some supervisors (to achieve an accomplishment) burn up their people. They mishandle their people. They use negative motivation and, therefore, have a heavy turnover. The focus must be on the people themselves. The accomplishment of the objective in a professional manner is important. We are interested in hiring Development Candidates who understand that keeping turnover low and morale high are extremely important. Again, you must be careful. You cannot tell us you do this. You must show us, quantifiably, how you motivate and interact with the people you supervise.

If your primary job objective is an engineering position, then show the recruiter your technical accomplishments. Always remember that your accomplishments must draw as close a parallel as possible to the position for which you are interviewing.

Quantifying Your Successes
As you build your resume, the extent of your success, the quantification of it, is the key factor. In order to know this quantification was successful, we have to know what the goal was. For example, if you reached a vehicle readiness factor of 95 percent, let us know this was three percent above objective, or whatever the case may be. Too many officers (as they interview with me) prove by their rhetoric that they probably should stay in the world of nonprofit. They constantly want to tell me how they developed a new training program. But, they never bother to tell me what the training program actually accomplished. **Once again, we are not interested in the front end of the accomplishment, only the back end.**

Officers say they designed a new transportation system, never bothering to tell me how that new system impacted the bottom line. They may tell me they designed a new software program, but again, they put their emphasis on the fact that they designed it— not what it accomplished. So, be careful that you learn what is important to the business world when discussing your accomplishments. Everything we do in industry must impact the bottom line of the company—saving man-hours, increasing profitability, lowering cost, etc.

Often, officers tell me, "I improved the morale of my unit." You need to show how it was done. What percent increase did you have in reenlistment? What percent decrease did you have in troops going AWOL? What decrease did you have in Article 15's? You must give quantifiable proof and evidence of what you say. Rhetoric alone won't suffice.

Some officers also tell me, "But, Roger, I spent $75 to get that resume built by a resume service." I'm sorry if I step on toes here. Too many times resume services are more interested in making a resume look pretty—focusing on how it's printed and the kind of paper used. I maintain that if these resume services charged you according to the success the resume produces, they might get more serious about the information they put on your resume.

Your resume must represent bottom-line qualities if you want a high degree of success in attracting companies to you.

Common Misconceptions

Many officers feel their resumes should be on the best bond paper. I agree, but the **content** is what's important. I've had recruiters tell me, "I don't care if they write it on paper grocery bags, as long as the content is right, and we can get the information we need."

I recommend two different resume formats. If you're leaving the military interviewing for a non-development position, it might be better to exclude extracurricular activities in high school and college. However, the majority of you will want to come to Corporate America and get into a development position. The major difference between the two resume formats is that one shows extracurricular activities in high school and college; the other does not. If you're interviewing for a development position and hope to be a top manager, keep in mind that most companies find top managers have successful traits in common, even in high school. As a Development Candidate, it's important, therefore, to show the extracurricular activities you had in high school and college. Over the years I've discovered these activities are very important—if you want a top leadership role with a major company.

The sample resume format I give you in Appendix D is for a development position and is a product of the many years I've spent recruiting officers and working daily with companies. I asked these firms the following question: What do you want to see in a resume to obtain the information you need? I want to note that I have been in a business where I am paid only for bottom-line performance, not for my opinion. This fact lends a lot of credibility to this resume format.

Most resumes should be held to one page (even those listing the backgrounds of LCDRs and Majors). But, don't be afraid to go beyond that if the information is relevant and presented in an articulate, succinct manner.

Resume Format Suggestions
The following resume format suggestions have been very successful for the candidates with whom we have partnered. I think you will find the resume format (as shown in Appendix D) to be an excellent one. Use this sample resume and the following guidelines to determine how to format your resume. Be careful and thorough, and create your resume using my instructions and resume sample as a guide.

- Use 1/2 inch margins for each side.

- Begin 1.7 inches from the top of the page. (If you are working with a recruiting firm, you may need to start lower to account for the firm's letterhead.)

- Single space your resume.

- Do not add more than one line between sections of the resume.

- Leave at least 1/2 inch at the bottom of the page.

- Use a 10-point professional-looking font.

- **Personal Information:** At the top left of your resume, place your full name, address, city, state, zip code, and your home phone number (including your area code).

- **Availability Date:** Approximately 4 1/2 inches from the left margin, place your availability date, written as month, day, and year. [Your availability date should be determined by subtracting your total amount of terminal leave (which you continue to accrue while on terminal leave) from your ETS, or last date of official service. **Be sure to use the earliest possible date.**]

- **Education Information:** This section should include all your undergraduate and graduate degrees and/or additional coursework. Place your undergraduate degree(s) on the left below your personal information and your graduate degree(s) and coursework below the availability date. [Your resume entries should match your college transcript entries for the degree(s) you were awarded. Many graduates have shortened their degree titles for convenience. **Refer to your transcripts to be sure of your degree title.** If you took a lot of courses in finance, that doesn't mean you had a minor in finance. If your transcript doesn't show it, don't put it on your resume. Some companies request transcripts, and if there is a discrepancy, it will be a significant strike against you.]

- **Activities:** Many of the candidates with whom we work have distinguished themselves not only academically but also in extracurricular endeavors. List both high school and college activities on the resume.

  For both high school and college, list the following: all scholastic honors and scholarships (except ROTC scholarships); honorary societies; student body government; class organizations; clubs; publications; assistantships; community, civic, or church memberships; and offices to which you were nominated or elected.

For any society, student body, class government, organization, or club in which you held an office or had a unique organization-specific accomplishment, include that office or accomplishment in parentheses following the entry. For example, "Debate Club (President, First Place State Forensic Tournament)."

For any athletic activity, annotate with "varsity," "junior varsity," "freshman," "club," or "intramural status" (mention only the highest level achieved). If you received awards or honors, enter them parenthetically as above. For example, "Varsity Football (Co-Captain, All-Conference, State Champions)."

If you have worked full-time or part-time in either high school or college, enter the following statement in the section(s) in which it applies: "Worked part- (or full) time, ____ hours per week, during _____ (school and/or summers)." Fill in the appropriate hours you worked. (Academy graduates should not include this statement in their college activities section.)

Immediately below the last line of your college activities section (do not skip a line) enter educational financing information. Type **"Note:"** followed by an explanation of how you paid for your undergraduate and graduate degrees. Determine how you financed your degrees—through full or part-time work (yours), your parents, scholarships (grants and other funding that were not repayable with scholarships), or loans. **Use percentages and be sure that funding types added together equal 100 percent.** Then, enter the percentages on the resume, starting with the largest percentage first. For example, "60 percent of undergraduate education financed by full-time work, 40 percent by loan."

• **Experience:** Below your educational financing entry, enter your **military** experience. Provide the dates of your active duty service, your military rank, your specialty, and your branch.

Next, enter your military work history. This is the most important part of your resume. Describe your duties and accomplishments for each position you held starting with the most recent job. For each position, enter four key elements:

1) *Date:* Enter dates of service by month and year.

2) *Job Title:* **For the vast majority of jobs, enter the technically correct title.** [Refer to your evaluations. Some job titles are not helpful to a recruiter, and you can't afford to spend your interview explaining what a title means. Therefore, you need to find a balance between what is technically correct (on your officer evaluations) and what is descriptive. **However, do not attempt to civilianize this or any other part of your resume.**]

3) *Job Responsibilities:* Enter three to five lines of information about your specific responsibilities for each job you list. (Refer to your officer evaluations. Be sure to include your supervisory responsibilities—number and type of personnel supervised. Be as specific as possible. The terms "mechanic," "electrician," "machinist," and "clerk" are more effective than "soldier." Also, discuss the amount and type of equipment for which you were responsible.)

4) *Accomplishments:* Enter the accomplishments you have achieved for each job you list. Each accomplishment

should stand on its own, in a "bullet" format. (Describe your accomplishments with action verbs. **Quantify your accomplishments**, or in other words, make your accomplishments measurable. For example, "Achieved a higher operational readiness rate" is too general and a matter of opinion. "Developed new maintenance program that achieved a 96 percent equipment operational readiness rate, 6 percent above objective" is a quantifiable accomplishment. It is specific and objective, rather than general and subjective.)

- **Civilian Experience:** Below your military experience, enter any jobs you have held as a civilian that may enhance your marketability. Begin your civilian experience as you did above for the military. Enter the dates, your title, and where you worked. Then, enter a description of your duties. (Do not detail your accomplishments; there will be no room for bullets in civilian experience. Areas you should include are the following: engineering, co-ops, lab assistantships, running your own business, computer work, or any job that relates to your experience. While we do not want to diminish the importance of these types of jobs, in terms of marketability, they are less relevant than your military career.)

Always carefully proofread and check your resume for errors (do not rely solely on spell check). Check all dates, making sure there are no time gaps or overlaps. Finally, read over your resume. Ask yourself this question, "Would you be interested in hiring this person to lead your company into the future?" If your answer is "no," go back and re-word your significant accomplishments. I am not suggesting you falsify accomplishments; I am suggesting you use language that is going to spark the interest of a corporate recruiter—language that will "sell" your ability to make an impact.

The Cover Letter

If you mail or in any way distribute your resume, it is crucial to send a cover letter along with it. The letter must be written specifically to that company. Do not send generic cover letters. You're telling the company all they need to know to decline you.

The resume must be able to stand on its own. Often, your cover letter will be removed from the resume when the resume is forwarded to hiring managers. The managers will be unaware of any cover letter. If you've put important information only in this letter, (and not duplicated it on your resume) it's likely to stay with the personnel director to whom you addressed it. Your resume will now be void of important data.

Make powerful statements in the cover letter. What can you offer that is relevant to that particular company? What are your abilities and career accomplishments? Why do you have a real interest in this corporation? Remember, keep the letter company-specific.

I consider your resume to be one of the most critical aspects of your job search. It's the primary factor, so build it first. You must have documentation on paper, listing who you are and what you're all about, along with your past performance. Too many individuals spend very little time on their resumes. What they produce simply isn't enough.

When you step in front of a recruiter for an interview, you want to know your resume has created a positive **first impression** about you and that the recruiter already has a positive attitude about you.

APPLICATIONS

Your application to a company (the actual application form) is a document that will represent you for the balance of your career if you go to work for that company. **Think about that.** It must be completed in a manner that you would always want in your permanent records.

This form may be the first impression a company representative has of you. Don't underestimate its importance. Think carefully as you complete the basic form. **Applications are designed to eliminate.** No company can interview everyone that fills out their application. However, I encourage you not to help them in the elimination process. I recommend you put yourself in the shoes of the corporate recruiter as you fill out any application. Reread it asking yourself, "Would I hire this person to lead my company into the future?" It could save both you and the company a lot of time going through a wasted interview.

Follow these basic rules:

1) Carefully follow the specific instructions on the application.

2) Type the application whenever possible, unless you are specifically instructed to do otherwise.

3) Check for correct spelling, correct grammar, and correct punctuation.

4) Don't leave blanks. If a question doesn't apply to you, put a short dash in the space, write "None," or write "N/A" (Not Applicable). Complete the entire form; don't skip questions.

5) Fill in the entire space provided for an answer. If, for example, there are three lines to list school activities, fill in all three lines.

6) **Never put "See Resume."** Company representatives know they can look at your resume. Your application must be able to stand alone and apart from your resume. It must clearly represent your entire experience and qualifications. Put all the information where the company wants it: on their application.

7) Avoid attaching an addendum or additional sheet. Although a form may state, "Feel free to attach supplemental information," the attached sheet can become detached—and then vital information will be lost. If there are four spaces provided for work history, and you had six jobs in the military, use two of the spaces for two jobs each. **Your entire military background should be divided so that all of your positions are included in the spaces provided.** Do not use just one space to indicate several years of military job experience, then the remaining three spaces for less notable work.

8) If asked to state "Reason for seeking change" or "Reason for leaving" a past or a present position, do give an answer. In the military, it may be due to promotion, change of duty, normal rotation, etc. But, your reason for leaving your current military position should be carefully worded. Don't say, "Completed military obligation." That shows no interest or conviction to make industry your career. State a positive, goal-oriented answer, such as, "Desire to pursue a career in major industry." **Use your own words.**

You'll find three caution areas that are especially sensitive subjects on many applications. Here's how to deal with them.

- **Salary.** Answer "Open" or "Negotiable." Please note this is not the way you would handle this question in an interview itself. But, an application cannot elaborate. It can't modify. You don't dare allow the application to get you ruled out because you put a dollar figure that doesn't allow latitude. This allows you to discuss the entire subject of compensation in person, with the company representative. It indicates salary is just one of many items you'll consider when making a career decision. If you must give a salary figure I recommend that you give a range, but hold it to $10,000. No one wants to see ranges of $30-40-50,000.

- **Location.** Always state "Open" on the application. **Again, this is completely different from what you would do in the interview itself.** If the word "open" is used in an interview, it will frequently disqualify you. If this question has two parts—"Do you have a preference?" and "Do you have any restrictions?"—answer the first by stating a broad geographical preference, such as "the Northeast," "the southern United States," "east of the Mississippi River," etc. Answer the second question, "None." If you know the location of the job for which you're interviewing, you can tailor your answer to that area. For example, you can state a preference of "east of the Mississippi" with "no" restrictions. It is reasonable to have a preference, but when the preference becomes an eliminator, then you should not plan to interview as a Development Candidate. National companies hire people they can promote without severe geographical restrictions. If you want to be a Development Candidate, you and your family must have a good attitude regarding multiple locations. If you were to suggest you wanted to go to the top 10 percent of any branch of the Armed Forces, you know you could not do so from a single location. Similarly, you can't get to the top 10 percent of Corporate America from a single location.

- **Position Desired/Objective.** Always state precisely the position title/objective. State only one objective per application, even if the application provides space for more than one position title.

The application is tangible, permanent evidence of your ability to answer specific questions and organize your ideas accurately and concisely.

CHAPTER 3

Preparing For The Interview

"I have known Roger Cameron for over 10 years, first as an Army Captain transitioning to Corporate America and now as a manager looking for world-class talent. Roger has captured the wisdom of his long experience in a concise text. You will benefit by being better able to articulate your strengths, experiences, and abilities in a way that will catch a company's attention and increase their interest. Just as you would check off your uniform in a mirror, you should check off your preparedness for an interview with **PCS to Corporate America**.*"*

— John M. Neilson
Director of Corporate Strategy
Miller Brewing Company

CHAPTER 3

Preparing For The Interview

What makes successful interviewing? That's simple—preparation. Preparation includes the following:

- A thorough understanding of yourself;
- A thorough analysis of what has made you successful; and
- The ability to communicate in a fluid, persuasive manner.

Sounds easy, doesn't it? But, it isn't. Many people feel they have the ability to take any subject matter and speak about it—"off the cuff"—in an articulate, concise, convincing manner. Unfortunately, few actually can. As a matter of fact, I'm not sure I've ever met anyone during my recruiting career—over two thousand officers a year—who found a position in the business world without serious interview preparation. Corporate recruiters are adamant that individuals prepare well for interviewing. As I mentioned in the Foreword, companies reason that if people do not work hard to prepare for something as valuable as their own careers, why should any company believe they're going to work hard to accomplish an objective for their employer? I believe this reasoning is very accurate.

If you want to succeed in your interviews, you will need to dedicate time to prepare for them. Set aside a specific period of time—an hour a day, two hours a day, five hours a week, one half-day a week, Saturday morning, Sunday afternoon—well in advance of interviews with corporate recruiters. Use this time to read books, to do work assignments, and to prepare for the key questions you know will be asked of you. I often use this example: If you knew you were going to have an inspection on Monday morning, you wouldn't begin preparing for it Friday evening. If you did, you certainly would know what the outcome would be. You wouldn't prepare on Friday evening for a six-month or a 30-day deployment, knowing that you're leaving on Monday morning. **Preparation is mandatory for quality results.**

FORTUNE 500 companies can go to the top college campuses in America and interview candidates with stellar track records (academics, extracurricular, etc.). They want the best of the best and can attract them as employees. These are the same companies who will interview you. You have to be at your best. You must meet their criteria and effectively communicate your track record. There's nothing automatic in the hiring process. The fact that you were good in high school, college, and the military does not automatically guarantee you a career in the business world. There's just that little thing called an interview that stands between you and success.

Think about it for a moment. You're over 27 years old and in an interview. You are being asked to communicate your life—your successes and failures, your strengths and weaknesses, what you are all about, and what you can offer a company—in a 30 to 45 minute period of time. No matter how old you are or how much experience you have to convey, company recruiters do not give you more time in an interview. It sounds absurd when you think about it, but this is exactly what will happen.

If you don't know what part of your experience a company is interested in (and chances are you won't), it stands to reason you must be prepared to give specific information on any part of your background at any time. It is the specific information that gets people without solid preparation into trouble. While you can talk in a general sense, you are rarely prepared to give the specifics of how you accomplished a particular event or objective.

Too many people feel being successful in an interview is about getting a resume together and buying a great suit and shoes, but that's only a very minor part of it. **The most important aspect of interviewing is being able to convince a recruiter that you have the objective and subjective skill set to make an immediate contribution to their company.** It is only when you communicate your skill set that they will see you as a good fit for their company. You cannot expect to do this without having a thorough understanding of yourself, of what has made you successful, and an ability to concisely and persuasively communicate this to the recruiter.

I've talked to many officers who interviewed with FORTUNE 500 companies without adequate preparation and never received offers. Consequently, without really wanting to, they stayed in the military. I honestly believe that, in many cases, they were declined by companies, not because of their credentials but because of their inability to communicate those credentials. It would be nice if you could get hired on the basis of a resume or an application, but it's just not possible. I've never known one of our client companies to hire a candidate sight unseen. So, please, dedicate yourself early in your career search to preparing for a very difficult venture—interviewing.

Objective And Subjective Assets
It is important for you to understand objective and subjective assets as you prepare for interviewing. Highlight or flag this section so that when you begin your actual preparation, you will start with this topic.

The cornerstone of self-evaluation is an understanding of your objective and subjective assets. When I ask officers during the interview process what assets they will bring to an employer on the first day, they often have no answer. Recruiters will ask this question in one form or another. It's important for you to understand the concepts in order to respond intelligently. Comprehension is critical to market yourself effectively.

Objective assets are points of fact regarding your background. This includes things like your degree, GPA, college, job experience, amount of time in leadership roles, number of people supervised, certifications, military schools, size of budgets you managed, etc. Objective assets are easily verifiable and make up the content of your resume.

Subjective assets are a different matter. Your subjective assets are characteristics, competencies, or behavioral traits, such as leadership, team building, initiative, self-confidence, integrity, attitude, organizational skills, creativity, problem solving ability, adaptability, perseverance, drive, out-of-the-box thinking, etc.

The business world conducts interviews to evaluate objective and subjective assets. If we were only concerned with objective assets, we would hire candidates simply from their resumes (a good representation of your objective assets). I see candidates all the time who have good credentials but weak subjective skills. These candidates struggle in their career searches, especially if they are competing for development positions.

All companies want a different collection of subjective and objective assets. These requirements change with different positions. A company will only value an objective or subjective asset if it is a requirement for the position. Many times, candidates make the mistake of emphasizing the wrong assets in an interview.

> **Objective Asset = Objective Value**
> **When the company requires the asset.**

To more fully understand **objective value**, let's say Company XYZ calls Cameron-Brooks to recruit engineers with leadership experience. In essence, Company XYZ is stating that, "objectively speaking," officers must have an engineering degree and leadership experience to interview with them. These two required assets are an **objective value** to Company XYZ. In addition to these two required assets, Company XYZ states that strong computer skills will be helpful but not required. If you have an engineering degree and leadership experience, you have the objective assets required to interview with Company XYZ. Now, let's say you are very computer literate, but your skills are not comparable to those of a computer science major. Your computer literacy will be considered **objective value-added**. Realize that what is value-added for one company may be required by another.

Let's consider this scenario: Ms. Hildebrand from ABC, Inc. wants us to recruit Development Candidates for her company. My first question is, "What are your requirements?" She says, "I need candidates with business degrees and GPAs of 3.0 or above—individuals who have participated in varsity sports or who were elected to leadership roles and who are able to start work by September 15." If you have these objective assets, you now have the qualifications to interview with ABC, Inc.

Ms. Hildebrand then reviews the subjective assets her company values. She says, "We're looking for individuals with a strong work ethic. I want someone who is willing to work hard to earn his or her pay. We insist on goal-oriented, 'make-it-happen' types." Ms. Hildebrand explains that goal-oriented, make-it-happen individuals are those who have a track record of setting demanding goals and who have the discipline to fight through adversity to accomplish those goals. In addition, her company wants people who are team players, who are creative, innovative thinkers, who are consensus-builders, who have vision, and who have pleasant personalities. This scenario is just one example. There are numerous variations of objective and subjective values depending upon the company and the position.

To prepare for the interview process, list all of the assets you possess that will be of value to companies. Remember that if the asset is required, it becomes valuable to the company. For most positions, your objective assets determine your functional value in the business world. **Your objective assets get you in the door and allow you to interview.** The more assets you have, the broader your marketability. It is really very simple:

> **More Objective Assets =
> More Doors of Opportunity**

Exceptions to this rule are sales positions that may require no specific objective value other than success in high school, college, and the military. In other words, the type of academic degree you have is immaterial. It could be any degree. In fact, the company recruiter may not even bother with objective assets but will concentrate only on your subjective assets. For some sales positions, a specific degree is important to have—for instance, when the product is very technical. In that case, a corresponding technical degree might be required. It would then be necessary for you to have an objective asset (technical degree) before you could interview with the company.

While objective assets will get you in the door, communicating subjective assets will get you hired. You could be a perfect objective fit for a company and still be ruled out in the interview (this happens all of the time). In other words, you could have the perfect academics and work experience, but if you cannot communicate the required subjective assets, you will not succeed in the interview. Therefore, your preparation for interviews also must include analysis of your subjective assets and, most of all, practice in communicating them. You should be able to describe your subjective assets with examples of accomplishments that illustrate the use of these assets. This is how you help company recruiters understand your methodology (your thought process behind getting things done, as well as behind the actual execution of goals and objectives), personality, attitude, and motivation.

What do you consider to be your strengths and distinguishing characteristics? Think in terms of what is most important to company recruiters. Refer to Appendix A for a list of key competencies (a compilation of subjective strengths and traits our client companies look for in Development Candidates) to help you determine your subjective assets. Companies want certain assets in potential hires, such as initiative, creativity, enthusiasm, being a team player, ability to communicate persuasively, conceptual and analytical skills, and interpersonal skills. Make sure your subjective assets are valuable to companies. Remember who "owns" the interview—the recruiter. If you want to be successful in the interview, as the interviewee, you want to be empathetic to the needs and interests of the recruiter. Put yourself in their shoes and ask yourself if you would hire you. Do you possess the subjective assets to get you hired? Help the recruiter fulfill his or her needs. **Too often interviewees fail in the interview because they are focused on what they want rather than on what the recruiter or company wants.**

After developing your list of subjective assets, take your five or six most important subjective assets and practice illustrating them in your answers to interviewing questions such as, "Tell me about a complex problem and how you solved it." "Tell me about a significant accomplishment and how you achieved it." Your answers to these questions should show your methodology—in other words, a recruiter should be able to visualize in his or her mind your method for doing things, your thought process behind accomplishing objectives and motivating others, and from your answer, a recruiter should be able to determine your subjective assets. To be successful in doing this, your answer must contain specifics. This is why preparation is so important. For you to go back two to five years or more and discuss specific details of how you accomplished a major objective is impossible without a lot of thought. Additionally, to articulate this in a persuasive and succinct manner (remember your time in an interview is limited) is impossible without a lot of practice.

The best way to practice articulating accomplishments and assets is to speak into a tape recorder and ask someone else to listen to the tape to determine how well you illustrated your assets. If the illustration is not clear to them, it will not be clear to the recruiter. You will find that to deliver your answers clearly, concisely, and effectively will take many tries.

Remember to be yourself in interviews. Maintain your individuality. Your experiences are yours. Your assets, objective and subjective, are yours. You are unique. You must be believable. The recruiter must see your strengths and be able to determine how well you will fit into his or her company. You must verbally create a picture that effectively illustrates your ability to join the company and make a significant contribution.

While the foundation of a successful interview is knowing your subjective and objective assets, you cannot get away with simply "laundry listing" those assets to a recruiter. The key is to show these assets in your examples of accomplishments. You must be able to consistently and persuasively articulate your assets by the examples you give in the interview. You also should carefully evaluate the recruiter's questions and tailor your answers to fit the specific job requirements. This means determining quickly in an interview which of your experiences is most relevant to the position for which you are applying.

General Store Analogy

An exercise that has proven to be beneficial in "translating" successes in your background into success in the interview is what we call the General Store Analogy. This preparation tool takes you to the next step by defining a method to effectively market your assets in the interview, much like a storeowner markets products in a store.

Think back to the western movies that showed a general merchandise store. The assorted products, such as nails, gloves, tools, buttons, thread, etc., were arranged in various drawers and cubbyholes in a shelving unit. The general store owner assisted customers with their shopping lists, matching their needs to products in the shelves. Each customer had a different request, and the owner was the product expert who would determine the best product for each individual need. No one knew the products better, and no one had more to gain from the sale. Customer service was the priority—a commitment to making sure customers were satisfied and their needs were fulfilled.

Now, picture your own general store. The product line consists of your objective and subjective assets. You have actually taken your asset list and stocked the shelves. You have many assets supported by examples and evidence to ensure your inventory is very marketable. Your customer (the company recruiter) enters your store with needs that you (the storeowner) must fulfill. You must evaluate and select the "best" product that matches or fits the company's requirements. Your selection and evaluation of the "best" product is critical. Just as the storeowner reviews and evaluates the customer's needs, so must you evaluate the recruiter's needs. After all, the storeowner would not sell a hammer to someone who wanted to paint a fence.

Your examples and evidence, concisely articulated, sell the products (your assets) to the recruiter. Remember: **No one knows the product better, and no one has more to gain from the sale.** Just as the general store owner wants to satisfy the customer's needs and sell their products, you want to "fit" the recruiter's needs and sell your assets!

Your ability to effectively match your assets to the recruiter's needs will be a key factor for success in your interviews. You see, the recruiter knows exactly what he or she is looking for in terms of a perfect "fit" for their company. You must have the ability to persuasively convince the recruiter that your total product (your objective and subjective assets) is **exactly** what the company needs!

Most people try to force the exact same objective and subjective assets on every recruiter. This works no better than the general store owner trying to sell the exact same merchandise to every customer. Customers all have different and specific needs—just like the recruiter. The general store owner must evaluate and identify each customer's needs in order to make the sale. You, too, must evaluate and identify each recruiter's needs to "fit" and sell your assets. When you understand and apply this concept to your interviewing skills, it has a powerful impact. Investing time and thought into the general store exercise can help you achieve a very smooth flowing exchange of quality and relevant information between you and the recruiter in the interview.

Developing Self-Insight
Client companies constantly ask me to bring them individuals who have the ability to look in the mirror, see exactly what's there, know who they are, and have the self-confidence to be able to tell a company what they're all about.

I am reminded of a time when I was evaluating an officer who, on his application under career objective, wrote CEO. Obviously, the minute he put this down as an objective, it was my job to see if there were proof and evidence that he could accomplish his objective.

I went back to his high school information to check how many times he had been evaluated number one. He hadn't graduated from high school as number one—he had a 3.1 GPA. I looked to see how many times he had been elected to leadership roles. There were none. His college GPA was 2.7. He was not president of his class, student body president, or, for that matter, captain of any athletic teams. I said, "Surely I'll find number one rankings in the military." I went to his military evaluations expecting, of course, to see only top-block evaluations. Again, there were some, but they were rather sporadic. I asked this individual one question: What do you feel are the odds you would be promoted to LCDR below the zone? He laughed at me. He suggested it would be very doubtful. With that, of course, I had to decline him. After all, if you can't be promoted below the zone to LCDR in the Navy where the statistics will actually be greater in your favor, it is unlikely you're going to leave the military and become CEO of a great company like Kraft Foods, General Mills, Corning, Guidant Corporation, Nextel or PepsiCo.

When I declined this individual, he said, "Roger that's not fair. You're suggesting that I shouldn't have high objectives." I looked at the young officer and said, "Please don't say that. You must have high goals. You must have goals that make you perspire—goals that make you use every asset of your being to accomplish them. But, they must be realistic goals." To become CEO can be a personal goal, but, in this case, it should never have appeared on his application. It will do you more harm than good. Remember, there is nothing wrong with ending up in the top 10 percent of a company's management structure. You do not have to be number one or two in the company to be successful. Have high goals, but be realistic and objective as to your ability.

Some officers I interview feel it necessary to say they are a 9 or a 10 in everything they do. If this assessment is not accurate, you could get yourself in a job you're not going to be able to handle. I encourage you to be realistic. The business world has the ability to recruit the very best from college campuses such as Harvard, Penn, MIT, Stanford, Northwestern, Duke, and other top schools across the country. Remember, we're accustomed to having the very best. You must compare yourself and your skills accurately to those people who are coming out of top schools with top GPAs. We know you have a great ability to perform, but we still want you to be realistic about the assets you bring to the business world. Companies are looking for people who are realistic about their abilities regarding job performance. **I can't count the number of officers I've seen ruled out because of inflated self-value. Remember this point.** Ambition is good, but keep it in perspective. We want to see confidence, not ego.

Discussing Your Weaknesses
As I interview officers, naturally, they want to talk about their positive attributes (strengths). Yet, recruiters also will want to talk about your less-than-perfect attributes (weaknesses), and most candidates haven't prepared themselves to discuss this topic. Great marketing companies in America have taught their sales people how to cover the negatives of a product. They spend as much time learning how to cover the product's negatives as they do covering the positives. Positives sell themselves and are fun to discuss, but negatives will cause you to be declined in an interview if they are not handled correctly.

One way to think about weaknesses is to analyze your strengths in relation to others. As you can see in the following graph, there are two strength lines: your normal strength line and your age group strength line. Your normal strength line is higher than the strength line for most people in your age group. There are those in your age group who did not finish high school, did not attend college, and have not had quality successes. The graph illustrates that any characteristic you would describe as "less than a strength" still would not qualify as a "weakness" as it would for most people in your age group. Those characteristics that are described as "less than a strength" are those that do not cause us to fail in the accomplishment of an objective. Recruiters won't ask you for "a less than a strength." They will ask for a weakness (or weaknesses). If you have a **consistent** weakness, do you really think they will hire you?

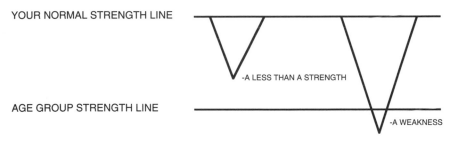

Now, how do you answer the question, "What are your weaknesses?" First, be honest. Hopefully, you can honestly identify a weakness. When you discuss it, use qualifiers such as "on rare occasions" and "very seldom." For example, if you feel you have an occasional problem managing time effectively, you could say, "On rare occasions" or "very infrequently." "There have been a couple of times I feel I could have better managed my time." You've been candid, but, in reality, have described an occasional "less than a strength" as a weakness. **By using strong qualifiers, you are leaving an important impression—that your weaknesses "rarely" or "seldom" present a challenge to the achievement**

of your objectives. Again, the key in discussing weaknesses is to emphasize the fact that you experience them infrequently.

Equally as important as using qualifiers to modify a weakness is to identify specifically what you are doing to overcome the weakness. Using the example of a weakness in time management, you could suggest a definite process you have established to ensure good planning. You might say, "I can specifically remember a couple of situations during my four years in the military that could have been more effectively managed. Now, each time I find myself in a planning mode, I walk through three specific steps. First, I focus on the objective of the event. Second, I coordinate the event activities to coincide with the time the event must be accomplished, and, third, I put solutions in place for any common problem that could interfere with the timely completion of the event."

Remember that the primary reasons recruiters ask you to discuss your weaknesses are to determine your ability to be honest and candid and to identify what you are specifically doing to correct your weaknesses. To communicate that you are always perfect is to be less than honest and will cause a recruiter to determine that you are not an open communicator (because we are all human and have imperfections) and could be cause for decline.

When you discuss your weaknesses, be careful that you do not preface your remarks by saying, "One of my weaknesses . . .." People do this frequently. When it occurs, a recruiter is forced to ask about and examine the other weaknesses that are inferred by this statement. This, obviously, will take away from the amount of time in the interview that you have to emphasize your achievements, because the recruiter is focusing on a discussion of your weaknesses.

Most weaknesses (such as difficulty remembering first names or ability to organize) are subjective, and most negatives (such as a low GPA or average military evaluation) are objective. I encourage you to be honest with yourself. Sit down and list anything that could be perceived as a weakness or negative in your background. Be thorough. Be practical. It is important to confront a negative. Don't brush it off. Don't push it to the side. Take time to examine the negatives and prepare your response. Some other examples of negatives might be an irrelevant baccalaureate degree, quality of the college, more than four years to get a college degree, or being on your fourth career decision at 26—law school, civil service, military, now Corporate America.

Preparing To Discuss Failure

It is critically important that you go into any interview prepared to discuss a failure. Remember that a failure is simply the non-accomplishment of an objective. It isn't necessarily earth shattering. It won't necessarily wind up on the front page of *USA Today*.

"Roger, I got caught off guard," a candidate sometimes says to me. "They asked me for a failure. I couldn't come up with one." **Don't let this happen to you.** There can be no excuse for that. You will be asked to discuss failures. There are two key factors about a failure that are important:

1) Companies want to see that you have enough self-confidence to be honest and forthright in describing a failure.

2) They also want to know what you learned specifically from the failure and what broad application this has for your future.

Companies will think if you have never failed that you've probably set your objectives too low. Before hiring, companies want to know how a candidate reacted to an adverse situation. More than one recruiter has told me that they want to see candidates who have crashed into a brick wall. Companies want to know how they've reacted—if they've **learned** from the failure. They actually have asked me not to show them candidates who have not failed. I absolutely agree, so be prepared to discuss a failure. And, don't be talked out of it. Once you've given a failure, accept responsibility for it, even if the failure was due to someone who worked for you. **Never attempt to justify the failure.**

The best example of failure you can give is one for which you were primarily responsible. It came from your lack of performance, inefficient time management, lack of organizational planning, lack of prioritizing, or overall ineffective management. **Remember that leaders do not justify failure—they learn from it.**

When you discuss a failure with a recruiter, explain **why** you failed, how you **reacted**, and what you specifically **learned**. What you learn should have broad applicability in the future. State how the failure encouraged you to improve skills in planning, organizing, communicating, analyzing, and delegating, but be specific. A recruiter wants to know that you can take an adverse situation and analyze how you would improve it, with or without a supervisor to tell you what to do. Recently, an officer told me that what she learned from a failure was that the next time she purchased specific component parts for her computer department, she would be sure to check with her boss to determine her pricing latitude. While it may have been the policy for her to check with her supervisor, she also could have analyzed her skills more thoroughly. She might have determined that she needed to be more detail-oriented or that she needed to improve her planning skills. The latter analysis is much more broad-based and can have a continuous positive impact on her career.

What Do You Do When Confronted With Failure?
This is a question recruiters often use as an eliminator. I encourage

you to look hard at it. It is a question that is similar to being handed a stick of dynamite with a one-inch lit fuse. Be careful of it. The key word in this question is, "confronted." The common response to this question is, "Well, the first thing I would do is analyze why I failed." Our response is, "But you haven't failed." What you've just told the company is, "The first thing I would do is proceed to fail, then I would turn around and analyze it." We don't think that is very smart.

Let's look at this situation for a moment. I explain to you, "You're coming to my hotel to interview with me. The road that you normally travel is blocked. Maybe it's being torn up to put in a new sewer system. Maybe a tanker truck turned over on it. What would you do?" You might say, "Well, I can't go down the road, so I'll turn around and go back home." Do you really? I doubt it. I think most of you would determine an alternative route to accomplish your objective. If I pointed that out, most of you would say, "Of course, that's what I would do." Yet, when we ask you what you would do, you talk about the failure.

The best answer to this question I have ever received came from an Army captain from Fort Bragg, North Carolina. I'll never forget her answer. She looked at me and, using hand gestures, said, "I can tell you one thing, Mr. Cameron—I wouldn't fail. If I can't get up the hill one way (she used her left hand to point), then I'll come up the other way (using her right hand to point a different direction)." I don't care what the specific words were, her answer was beautiful. She wasn't going to allow any barrier to stop her.

Recruiters from all of our client companies have said to me that they want people who can **make things happen**. They explain, "I don't want you recommending people to me who, the minute the going gets tough, simply throw up their hands and accept the failure. That is not what we're looking for. We want people who can work through difficult situations, solve problems, and drive an objective through to successful completion."

On a recent trip to the Norfolk area, I asked this question of an officer I was interviewing there. The officer looked at me and gave me an answer that I hear far too frequently. The individual said, "The first thing I do when I am confronted with failure is reanalyze the objective." In other words, he will analyze his objective and lower it. If all we had to do was to lower our objective every time we were confronted with failure, nobody would ever fail.

Another frequent response is, "Well, the first thing I do when confronted with failure is let my boss know of a pending failure." My response is always the same. "Be glad you do not work for Roger Cameron, because that's only going to happen one time. I hire people to lay solutions—**not problems**—at my feet."

To go through this book and simply learn answers to questions isn't what this book is all about. I expect you to analyze yourself and ask, "Am I really a make-it-happen type of person? When I confront failure, do I do something about it? Does my mind automatically find an excuse to rationalize why it is okay to fail? Or, do I figure out a different solution to accomplish the objective?" If it isn't the latter, do yourself a favor and stay out of the business world. It is an extremely competitive environment—more competitive than ever today. Those people who do not have the ability to find solutions to difficult tasks will fail.

Imagine a top FORTUNE 500 company coming to me and saying, "Roger, we would like to pay you a fee to travel around the world and find us people who, when confronted with problems, give them back to us." Wouldn't that be absurd? Quite the contrary, companies come to me and say, "Roger, bring me people who can put in place solutions for difficult issues." I can never comprehend hiring anybody and paying him or her an outstanding salary to lay problems at management's feet. Don't miss this loaded question. Be careful. The question can be asked many ways using many different words. It won't necessarily be asked as obviously as I've asked it. It's the concept you must understand.

A Word About GPA

Everyone we hire in the business world can't have a grade point average of 3.8 or 4.0. It would be nice, but it's unrealistic. Is there anything wrong with a low GPA? Maybe. If you don't have the ability to convert the GPA into outstanding performance, then, yes, there's something wrong with it.

I want you to realize we consider GPA to be an **indicator**. It's not absolute proof of your ability to perform. It's an indication that you're going to be an average or above-average performer, depending on the GPA. But the real proof of your abilities lies in your performance evaluations as an officer. We ask this question: Can the GPA be converted to bottom-line performance? Unfortunately, I've seen officers with high GPAs who were unable to do this, and I have worked with some absolutely outstanding candidates who had relatively low GPAs. One young man, for example, had a 2.0 GPA, but every one of his evaluations was outstanding. He was consistently rated by his superiors as the best they'd supervised. He was able to convert the knowledge he gained from academics to bottom-line military performance. Under no circumstances am I suggesting you be casual about a low GPA, but I want you to understand how Corporate America uses GPA to evaluate candidates. In the business world, education is considered a tool, not a ticket, and, therefore, a relatively low GPA will not necessarily prevent you from coming to Corporate America as a Development Candidate.

Never justify a low GPA. I recall an officer I interviewed at Fort Lewis, Washington. When I asked about his low GPA, he said his priorities were simply in the wrong place. I said, "If you were to go back and do it over, would you do it differently?" He replied, "No, I don't feel I would." And, with that, I declined him. Here's the analogy I drew: A young man worked for me. I sent him out on a job to accomplish a given objective. Then, he came back with average to poor performance. We had a conversation as to how it could have been better. I asked him, "Now, if you had the opportunity to do that job again, would you do it differently?" He told me, "No." I said, "You've got to be kidding." **So, be careful with suggesting that, in retrospect, you would still achieve only poor or fair performance. Never defend poor performance.**

We gain different perspectives as we mature and grow older. Therefore, you wouldn't go back and do everything the same. We realize, for example, that the purpose of college is academics, not extracurricular activities. Square your shoulders and simply admit that you didn't accomplish what you had the capability of doing. You'd like the opportunity to go back and redo it. But, that's not possible, so explain (and give evidence) that you've been able to convert your low GPA into quality performance on the job. Some of you also can point to more recent academic achievements (advanced degrees, certifications, etc.) where you demonstrated a better ability to apply yourself intellectually.

Handle your GPA head-on. Don't back away from it. And, don't say you went to college to be "well-rounded" and therefore your social life and extracurricular activities necessarily detracted from the effort you put into your studies. I've known many outstanding individuals with GPAs of 3.7 and higher. I can assure you they were extremely well-rounded. It won't work to suggest that because you have a low GPA, you're well-rounded and the person with a high GPA is not. That's an alibi that will not stand up in the eyes of a recruiter. Don't explain away a low GPA.

Confront it. It had to be either a question of poor judgment or a question of intellect. Let's hope it was the former.

Asking Quality Questions

Asking questions during an interview is equally as important as your ability to answer questions. You will be judged on your intelligence; your comprehension of the job, the company, and the industry; your ability to express yourself; and your ability to ask questions that will get the information you need.

Curious people ask questions. They are interested in what is happening and becoming more knowledgeable. We want people who are curious. When you ask questions, you get answers. When you get answers, you become more knowledgeable. You demonstrate that you have a desire to learn and that you are a growable person.

Asking quality questions is an opportunity for you to demonstrate your understanding of and interest in the position for which you are interviewing. Your questions will show your intellect. They will show your interest. Your questions can help further establish rapport between you and the recruiter. These are important issues in any interview.

Think about it this way. If you were interviewing someone for a position, what kind of questions would you like to see from a potential hire? Naturally, you would judge the candidate by the quality of his or her questions. Do they show a genuine interest in the company? Do they seem fascinated with this work? Do they seem intrigued with the company? Are they enthusiastic about the opportunity?

Please don't shrug this off. Don't think questions will come to mind when you get into an interview. I can tell you this gives candidates as much or more difficulty than any other aspect of interviewing. You have to prepare quality questions before you go into the interview.

Good questions can be formulated from the job description and corporate recruiting literature (sometimes given to you prior to the interview or available on company web sites). These are great sources for developing questions. Carefully read the job description and the company literature for what it does not tell you. Make a practice out of reading everything for both what it tells you and what it doesn't tell you. One of the best ways to do this is to take the company literature and write down questions as you read. If you don't do it this way, you might run into an embarrassing situation by asking a question that has been answered in the literature. This can be devastating to a quality interview as it is a definitive indicator that you did not do your homework. The recruiter says, "The candidate doesn't even have the professional courtesy to read our recruiting literature." In essence the candidate is saying, "I don't care enough to read the literature. I just want to go ahead and ask the questions." Be careful! Read the literature. Study the company's website. Both will prompt you to think of several relevant, quality questions.

I recommend that you prepare two to three open-ended questions before you go into an interview. When the opportunity to ask a question arises, you will be prepared but you need not solely rely on this list. Listen and focus on what the recruiter has to say and more questions will come to mind. Most people ask one question and then as the recruiter is responding, they are trying to recall the next question they have on their list. Wrong, wrong and wrong. Let me create a correct scenario for you. Sally (corporate recruiter) calls our President, René Brooks, and asks her how our last conference performed. René says, "It was outstanding in that it produced the highest ratio of pursuits to interviews and some of the highest offers in the history of our company." Now watch how a person with curiosity can develop a point by asking good questions, (which is exactly what you must do when you get to your interviews).

Sally says, "René, to what do you attribute this success?" René responds; Sally listens. Sally's next question: "Is this a trend you see continuing and if so, why?" René responds; Sally listens. Her next question is, "Do you find that all industries are hiring or just a few?" René responds; Sally listens. And the process continues. Sally stayed focused on René's answers; by asking more questions she developed a picture that had depth; by the time the conversation was over, Sally also had valuable information. René was pleased because of Sally's sincere interest and ability to listen. Having interest is a compliment, which René also enjoyed. Rapport was further developed between Sally and René. Practice asking good questions. Engage yourself in what others have to say and get information out of conversations.

During initial interviews, only ask questions related to the position you are seeking. You want to show interest in the position (after all, if you ever go to work for the company, this job is what you will do every day). Ask open-ended questions that will help you understand the nature of the position. Your questions about benefits, locations, promotions and other non-job related issues should always be reserved for follow-up interviews.

Take the position and break it into its component parts. For example, if you were interviewing for an Information Technology position, you might want to ask questions about the company's high priority IT projects, their objectives, and the technologies involved. By doing so, you will uncover the specifics on the type of work you will do and thus help you connect your abilities and experiences to the job requirements.

For a sales position perhaps the breakdown could include the following: product and customer. For production: equipment, maintenance, and people. In an interview, focus on one component at a time, then move to the next issue. Your questions should follow a natural progression or sequence of thought. Remember, all questions you ask should strictly relate to the particular job for which you are interviewing.

One way to develop good questions is to picture yourself going to work the first day. Think of all of the things you don't know about your new job. Focus on details. Develop questions that will clarify this picture in your mind.

Your questions should never be generic. They should be company-specific. It is very impressive in your interview to show due diligence in your homework. For instance, the following remark shows the candidate did her research: "I read in your annual report that last year the company successfully implemented a high performance team concept. Can you tell me more about this initiative?" You can see the positive impact this statement of fact (and something that could not be said to any other company) would make on a recruiter. When you do this, the question is being asked specifically about that company.

Candidates have asked in interviews, "What new products are you bringing to the market?" They've got to be kidding. Companies will not take somebody off the street and tell them what they're doing in research and development. New products are the biggest secrets companies have. This kind of question shows poor judgment. Can you imagine going to the Iraqi Army and saying, "What new weapons are you developing?" They would laugh at you. You're smart enough not to do that. You must also be smart when you interview with companies.

You might find it useful to use numbers in forming your questions. Here are good examples: "Can you tell me the two biggest process improvement initiatives? Can you tell me the top two challenges your company faces in keeping its market share?" In other words, by asking about one or two factors, you really are inquiring about the most frequent or most significant.

For example, "How will I be evaluated in your company? In the military, I'm evaluated usually by two people—my immediate rater and my senior rater. They evaluate me on a host of different factors: my written and oral communications skills, my maturity, and knowledge of my job. I'm curious. What are the top three performance criteria for the employees of your company?" Take the time to design your question and formulate it (in relation to your historical background) so the recruiter can better address the question.

As always, be mindful of time. Don't ask questions the recruiter will need 10 to 15 minutes of your 45-minute interview to answer. The recruiter is not going to accept you on the basis of his or her answers, but on the basis of your answers. While it is important for you to ask quality questions, it also is important to use good judgment in asking questions that can give you information you need but be answered in a concise, succinct manner.

I recently interviewed an officer for 25 of his 30-minute interview. I had previously stated at my Information Meeting that at the conclusion of their personal interview I would tell all officers whether I could or could not facilitate their move to Corporate America. At the end of 25 minutes and the end of my questions, I asked this officer if he had questions. He said, "No, there is nothing I can think of." So, I got up, opened the door, and let him out. I suppose he's still wondering if he was accepted. Should he ever read this book, he will know the answer. But, can you really imagine someone filling out an application, leaving work, driving to my hotel, interviewing for 25-30 minutes, driving home, and never determining if he accomplished his objective? Wow!

Never suggest you don't have questions. Intelligent, curious people always have questions.

I recall a candidate we had who did really well with a company at the Career Conference and traveled to a follow-up interview at the company headquarters. The company raved about the candidate and wanted to give him an offer. Because one key manager was unable to interview the candidate during the follow-up, the company scheduled a telephone interview between this manager and the candidate (mostly as a formality before giving the candidate an offer). Unfortunately, the candidate forgot the importance of asking good questions and was ruled out. The recruiter just could not believe that a person interested in his company would end an interview without asking some good questions. It did not matter how qualified the candidate was, lack of quality questions ruled the candidate out.

Sometimes, a recruiter will use virtually the entire interview and leave you only a couple of minutes to ask questions. Be careful. Just because you are getting close to the end of the interview, you should not say, "I have no questions." This will come across as a negative. A better way of handling it might be, "Yes, I have other questions, but none I need answers to at this time. I can already tell you, I have a very strong interest in your company, and I'll save my questions to be answered in my follow-up interview." Remember, this is only if you are out of time. This is not a license to forgo questions.

I also know recruiters who like to begin the interview by asking for your questions. Yes, that is right. They will let you start the interview with your questions. They do this because it is an easy way to differentiate candidates (again by the quality of your questions). You need to be prepared for this type of interview as it is virtually impossible to rescue the interview if you start off with obviously low weight questions like, "What is a typical day like?" I have seen this happen hundreds of times.

Asking Negative Questions
Some of the questions you might ask are what we call negative questions such as, "Could you give me insight into your turnover factor? Could you tell me why your quarterly earnings were down 10 percent? Could you tell me about the tenure of your labor force? What percentage of your products is returned because of poor manufacturing quality? What percentage of your products is delivered to the customer on time?" These questions could have a good foundation for asking. However, they must be asked in a manner that will not come across as negative and suggest to the recruiter that you are a cynical person.

Deliver questions in a positive way. I recommend something like the following: "I'm sure a company of your quality strives for top financial performance. Could you give me some insight into your recent financial results?" Make the tone of your questions positive. Take time to develop questions. Word them so they are not negative.

I hope I've made my point. You must be serious about doing your homework and being prepared to ask quality questions.

Researching Companies
I'm frequently asked about the importance of doing research on companies before interviewing with them. Please don't confuse this with doing research on business practices and trends. Being knowledgeable about the business world is imperative (after all, we want to believe you have made an informed decision and that you have a basic understanding about the type of environment in which you plan to pursue your future career); however, the importance of doing research on companies prior to your inter-views depends on two things. It depends on whether or not you

are working with a recruiting firm and where you are in the hiring process.

If you are working with a recruiting firm, check with the firm first. It is usually not necessary to thoroughly research specific companies prior to attending a given career conference. A quality recruiting firm should supply you with definitive information about the particular company, position, and recruiter for each of your interviews. We supply our candidates with more pertinent information than they could ever find on their own.

If, on the other hand, you're going to send out resumes and interview with a company on your own, you must research that company thoroughly. Call the company and ask them to send you literature. Tell them you are coming in for an interview and would like to read and study the literature ahead of time. Visit the company's web site and conduct research on the company via the Internet. While this research will give you general information about a company, what is really needed for a successful interview is specific information about the position and/or functional area for which you are interviewing. You need to be able to relate your background and experiences to the requirements and responsibilities of the position. If you know someone within the functional area for which you are interviewing and they are willing to give you specific information, this might be a good way to acquire information. Please keep in mind, however, that this information is a matter of opinion and should not be considered statements of fact.

For initial interviews, research is necessary to help you understand job requirements and responsibilities and formulate quality questions. **However, while this information is important, what you know about yourself is more important than what you know about the company.** At our Career Conferences, candidates will have structured interviews in which interviewees communicate information only about themselves. Many recruiters have said to me, "I don't really care what candidates know about us. I want to know what they know about themselves. What can they articulate to me in a concise manner in a 30 to 45-minute interview? I want to learn about them." The most critical research you need to do prior to your initial corporate interviews is research on yourself. Have the ability to communicate that knowledge to a corporate recruiter.

Now, once a second or what we call "follow-up" interview is scheduled, you must research the company thoroughly whether you are working with a recruiting firm or on your own. Read the annual reports. Read the corporate literature. Visit the company's web site. Use the Internet to find relevant information on the industry, the company's products, etc. Demonstrate an interest in the company. If it is a consumer-oriented company, go to a retail store and look at their product and how it's merchandised. If it is a telecommunications company, talk to some of their customers about the company's services. We like to see candidates who are resourceful enough to research the company in unique ways before their follow-up interview with that company.

Colloquialisms And Qualifiers
Officers win the gold medal for using qualifiers! No one is as expert at using the qualifier as is the military officer. I have no idea where it comes from. "I think." "I believe." "Probably." You must understand that the minute you give any type of answer with a qualifier in it, your answer is immediately eliminated. What you've said to the recruiter is, "I'm not really sure, but here's what my guess would be." In an interview we're not asking for your guess, we're asking for the way it is.

I remember I had a young recruiter working for me. I became very frustrated with him over a period of time. It was time to sit down and have a nose-to-nose conversation. He consistently used qualifiers in answering the simplest of questions. I had asked him what time it was. He looked at his watch and said, "I **think** it's **about** . . . .," instead of looking at his watch and saying, "It's 1:09." In other words, he used two qualifiers just to tell me what time it was! As I say, it was nose-to-nose time!

Do not use words such as "yeah," "you know," and "roger," or "check" for "yes." There is absolutely no reason for you to ever use the words "you know." I quickly remind people that if "we knew," we wouldn't be asking the question.

I remember one individual who began and ended every sentence with "okay." This is not something you can do and call yourself a good communicator. Be very careful of colloquial expressions and qualifiers.

Involving Spouses/Significant Others
Should spouses (or significant others) get involved in a career search? Absolutely! In all the years I've been in this business, I have encouraged spouses/significant others to attend our Information Meetings, Personal Interviews, and Career Conferences. Changing career direction is one of the most important moves you're going to make in your lifetime. It affects the futures of you and your spouse/significant other. Your career is probably the longest relationship you will have next to marriage.

Examine this critical move as a team. Our Information Meetings include too much information to take home and give in proper context to someone else. Your spouse/significant other needs to be involved in gathering and analyzing information so you can make an informed decision together. You both should have the same degree of knowledge regarding the business world, and you both should have the same degree of commitment to making your lives and career(s) in the business world successful. Spouses/significant others can offer constructive critiques and help with interview preparation. They also should be involved when you are evaluating offers and making a decision about a position and the company with which you will launch your business career.

When spouses/significant others help with interview preparation, they need to be very honest in their critiques. At the same time, they need to be highly supportive and give lots of positive reinforcement. Effective interviewing is difficult (remember you must be at your best), and preparing to be at your best can be very frustrating. This is not the time to be nice or let things slip by. Offer help constructively. If you are too casual in giving critiques when your spouse interviews with a recruiter, there is the tendency to do or say the same incorrect things. While frustrating for interviewees, spouses/significant others must mention every time a word is misused. Point out when your spouse rambles, implies but doesn't state, and when he or she says, "you know." Spouses/ significant others should be particularly aware of the believability of the delivery. If answers don't sound sincere, I can assure you the recruiter will sense the same thing.

Spouses/significant others should ask themselves, "Do I understand exactly what my spouse is saying? Does my spouse come to the point immediately, give me substance, and answer the entire question? If I were a recruiter, would I like the way the answers were delivered? Is there enthusiasm in the voice and a sparkle in the eyes? Will my spouse excite the listener? If I were a recruiter, would I want to hire my spouse?" Detach yourself. Be a strict and thorough evaluator. Demand quality performance. It is the only way to help your spouse/significant other improve his or her interviewing skills.

Talk into a tape recorder. You and your spouse/significant other can then better evaluate what is said. Sometimes, you will want to defend yourself, saying, "That isn't what I said," or "That isn't how I meant to say it," or "I don't think that's what I said." The tape recorder will play back exactly what you've said and won't lie to you. If you can't articulate or deliver smoothly into a tape recorder, you will not verbalize effectively in front of a recruiter either. These are frustrating methods of preparation, but frustration in front of your spouse, a tape recorder, or, for that matter, your recruiting firm, will not cost you an interview. Frustration in front of a company will probably cost you a follow-up interview and a job offer.

If working with a spouse/significant other is not possible, work with other officers who also are making a transition. Ask your recruiting firm for names of those on your base or in your area who are preparing for corporate interviews or an upcoming career conference. Work with these individuals. Make a pact to be honest in critiquing one another. Be willing to throw out ideas. Everyone stands to benefit from group work sessions. The sessions will force you to practice articulating accomplishments, and you will receive valuable feedback.

Talking In The First Person
In the military as in the business world, the most dominant pronoun used to describe actions is "we." However, in an interview when describing actions and answering questions the only correct pronoun to use is "I." **"I" is the only word in the English language that gives you total ownership of an action.** "We" shares the action and "you" assumes a philosophical stance or discussion. Please, bend the corner of this page. Highlight every word in this paragraph. The recruiter is interested in knowing about you—not anyone else. He or she doesn't want to know what you might do in theory but rather exactly what you do in reality. This concept is critical to a successful interview and is difficult for most officers to adopt. You must develop the habit of talking in the first person (using the pronoun "I") long before your first interview.

As we accomplish missions in the military and in business, it is only professional to share the success. However, when you are being interviewed, the recruiter is only interested in hiring one person for each position. Therefore, if you sit in front of a recruiter using the pronoun "we," you will fail in the interview. First of all, the recruiter is not interested in hiring all of "we," and, second, it is going to be difficult for the recruiter to siphon out what **you** did. If your accomplishment was a group success, you might describe it this way: "My accomplishment was ———. We were successful because I had some great soldiers working for me. Each member of our team made this accomplishment happen. Without them I could never have had the same degree of success. My role in this mission was———." Now you proceed in the first person. I planned; I organized; I created; I motivated; I persuaded, etc. Imagine yourself as a puppeteer. You are orchestrating the actions. The key is to give sincere credit to your team while making clear your role, abilities, and responsibilities related to the accomplishment.

Be careful not to be too "I" oriented. Give credit where credit is due. Show that you know the importance of taking care of your team members and that you exercise this. If you don't, you will be ruled out for coming across as being egocentric.

Spouses/significant others, here is a great way to make some money. Fine your spouse/significant other every time he or she uses the pronouns "we" and "you" when they should be using "I." Begin with a $1 fine for each misuse, and, if that doesn't work, raise the fine to $5. I cannot emphasize enough the importance of developing this habit early in your preparation process. If you wait to practice talking in the first person when it is time to start interviewing, it will be too late.

DON'T USE MY WORDS.
USE MY THOUGHTS.

Make sure the answers you give are your answers. Make sure they are well thought out and represent an accurate picture of yourself and your skills. The end result of preparation is that you have intellectualized your answers. You understand yourself, your abilities, your accomplishments. The next step is to deliver them with passion and conviction in an interview. **Passion indicates ownership and believability.** Be careful—don't miss this point. All the preparation in the world is worthless unless the recruiter believes your answers are genuine.

Developing A Habit Of Professional Reading
As a Development Candidate in Corporate America you will be expected to read everything you can get your hands on. Reading for professional development must be a habit, like brushing your teeth in the morning. We want people who like to grow their knowledge base and who understand the importance of doing so. We want people who have a high degree of curiosity. We never believe you're too busy to read. Make reading of diverse subjects a habit!

I no longer ask my audiences if they read business periodicals, national newspapers or books that have been on the best seller list for months and months. I have found that few military officers read a wide variety of subject matter. Many of you read a lot of military publications and while that is good, we would like to see you read a wide array of material, especially if you are planning to transition to the business world.

You must continue to grow intellectually if you want to consistently achieve. Our client companies demand we bring them

---

knowledgeable people who are willing to grow. Pick up a book for 30 minutes before going to bed at night. If you tell me, "I don't have time to do this," I think you need to reevaluate your career and your life. You cannot spend the rest of your life in a formal academic environment. Therefore, you must read in order to gain knowledge.

A critical part of your transition preparation must include gaining an understanding of the business world and the different careers available to you. You must be able to communicate this understanding intelligently in an interview. Listed in the back of this book in Appendix B are sources I recommend for your personal development and specifically, to gain business knowledge. This list is not exclusive, but suggests reading material to help you gain a broad knowledge of the business world and thus be better prepared for corporate interviews and a successful business career.

Getting Organized

I've never observed a highly successful person who wasn't organized. Successful people are able to juggle numerous appointments, assignments, responsibilities, and dates to remember and still meet their obligations within difficult time limits. Learning to be thoroughly organized should be part of your early development. I see many military officers who do very well at this; however, some do not. Don't wait until others see you as unorganized and forgetful before you develop the professional habit of organizing and planning your time efficiently. I can attest to the fact that some Development Candidates have had setbacks in their careers for just this reason.

I strongly recommend you purchase a planning system. There are many different planning products and systems from which to choose, ranging from hand-held computers to software programs to hard-bound planning systems. Most desk and laptop computers now come installed with contact and time management tools, as well. The hand-held and palmtop devices are becoming increasingly popular because of their size, portability and capability. In addition to time and contact information management, these devices allow you to reference information, word process, and e-mail. Listed below are a few web sites I recommend you explore to learn more about each of these highly effective planning systems and tools:

- www.daytimer.com (Day-Timers, Inc.);
- www.dell.com (Dell Computer Corporation);
- www.franklincovey.com (Franklin Covey Co.);
- www.hp.com (Hewlett Packard);
- www.palm.com (Palm Computing); and
- www.zones.com (Mac Zone).

Your Mission

Company recruiters consistently compliment us on how prepared and knowledgeable our candidates are. We work very hard to effectively prepare, teach, develop and coach our candidates. Some clients describe our development program as a mini-MBA. Our candidates read every book they can. They learn everything they can about themselves. They learn the best way to have successful interviews. They practice, practice, and practice! These officers make it their mission to maximize their market-ability and earn as many interviewing opportunities as they can. In fact, this is exactly the way companies will expect you to approach an objective you attempt to accomplish in your business career. They will expect you to prepare well, do thorough research, and then execute with precision. You cannot expect a recruiter to believe you will prepare well and work hard to accomplish missions for their organization when you haven't done the same for your own interviews and future professional career!

By conducting a great interview, you will show the recruiter that you prepare well and work hard to accomplish your objectives. A career transition is as deserving of preparation as every other important mission in your life—if not more so.

> **THE SECRET OF SUCCESS IS DOING WHAT YOU OUGHT TO DO, WHEN YOU OUGHT TO DO IT, WHETHER YOU WANT TO OR NOT, NO DEBATE.**
> **— Walter Hailey, Jr.**

The Physical Factors Of Interviewing

"Getting out of the military and going into the corporate world is a stressful time. Roger gives you a roadmap for success with his advice and wisdom in **PCS***. We continue to use Roger's candidates for our needs across the country because they are the best. Roger will help you prepare for a very rewarding career in Corporate America. Read and take heed because Roger knows what it takes to be successful in today's environment."*

— Bill Quilici
Western Regional Sales Director
Ethicon Endo-Surgery, a division
of Johnson & Johnson

CHAPTER 4

The Physical Factors Of Interviewing

Clothes And Appearance

Once you start to work for a company, you'll be measured primarily according to your performance. When you interview, you're going to be judged on every possible factor, including what you wear. It's sad to hear of someone who has worked hard to secure a good education, build an impressive resume, put in time preparing for interviews, and is ruled out because of the way he or she is dressed.

If you're outstanding and have done everything right, it's possible, but doubtful your clothes will rule you out of a job—unless they are unprofessional. But, if the recruiter feels something about you is questionable and that is compounded by a poor appearance, then your clothes will become a major factor. I recommend that you read John Molloy's *Dress For Success* (for men or women). Acceptable business attire for men has been established and widely practiced for many years. On the other hand, business attire for women is not universally understood, and women can easily make serious mistakes when they take advice from well-meaning people (even clothing store personnel) who do not understand what constitutes professional business clothing for women. Therefore, it is very important for women to read Molloy's *Dress For Success For Women*. The best rule of thumb for men and women to remember regarding appearances in the entire interviewing and hiring process is this:

Your physical appearance should imply that you are professional and competent and that you can get the job done. This does not mean you should look dull, but, if you err, it should be on the side of being conservative versus highly fashionable. Remember that you are not trying to please your friends or the fashion experts but rather the people who make hiring decisions. These individuals are usually older and conservative (at least in their business appearance), and care more about what you can accomplish than how good-looking you are.

Please note that my recommendations for dress are solely for the purpose of success in the corporate interview. I'm not attempting to address what you should wear on the job but only what you should wear in the interview. Once you are in a business career, you will have greater flexibility to dress as you please.

We recommend that women have two suits for interviewing purposes. Each suit should have matching jacket and skirt and should be designed in a traditional, conservative style, in solid colors of either navy blue or dark gray. Some national brands we recommend are Harvé Bernhard, Austin Reed and Jones of New York. Many styles and colors are available in women's business suits today, and you must select suits of traditional cuts and colors for interviewing. Women should not wear pin stripe suits or men's ties or try to look like men. The length of the skirt should be at the knee or just below the knee to two inches below the knee. White or off-white tailored blouses are best. They should not be sheer, overly lacy, or made of a fabric commonly worn in social situations. The neckline should be discreet and professional in appearance.

Shoes should be low-heeled (two inches or less is a good rule of thumb) with closed toes and heels. You should be able to stand easily and walk briskly in your shoes. Black, navy, or other dark neutral colors are best. Wear natural-colored hose with no seams or texture.

A woman's handbag should be of small or moderate size and only large enough to carry essentials. It should be what we call "a business purse" that simply gets the job done. Again, black, navy, or dark neutral colors are best.

These points are also important for women: Keep your jewelry to a minimum for an interview. One ring on each hand (at the most) and a strand of pearls or a simple gold chain is sufficient jewelry. If you wear earrings, they should be small or fit close to the earlobe. Dangling earrings are not appropriate.

Women should have a hairstyle that is neat and professional. If your hair is below shoulder length, wear it pulled back—in a chignon or French braid. A tailored hairstyle is best.

Your make-up should be light—blush and lipstick that are natural looking rather than bright or dramatic. Avoid heavy eyeliners or shadows. Your fingernails should be medium to short in length. If you wear nail polish, be sure it is clear. Keep perfumes light or wear none at all.

For both men and women, the rule is to look conservative, professional, classic, and sharp. Everything should be done in moderation. That's why overdoing perfume or aftershave lotion can leave a reminder of you long after you're gone—and not in a positive way.

I have no idea why anyone would come to an interview with an alarm clock—whether it's a Big Ben you put on the recruiter's desk or a wristwatch you wear on your arm. If I'm in the middle of an interview and the candidate's alarm goes off, it is very disrupting. I also consider it very unprofessional. If you need a watch that tells you every time the hour or the half-hour strikes, that's fine, but turn it off or remove it before you come to an interview.

While a recruiter for a major national company was interviewing an officer, the candidate's wristwatch alarm went off. The recruiter got up from behind his desk and said, "Obviously, you have something more important than this interview," walked the young man to the door, and let him out. I don't blame him. It's highly inconsiderate to allow an alarm to go off during an interview.

Though the sports watch look is popular today, it is too heavy and bulky and does not look appropriate with a business suit. If you wear a watch for your interviews, wear one that is professional looking, understated and appropriate for business attire.

In stressing light jewelry for all male candidates, I suggest nothing more than a class ring, a wedding band, and a business-style wristwatch.

Men's hair should be cut in a conservative, professional style. If you have a hairstyle that parts, be sure your part is clean and well defined. If your hair is very fine and has a tendency to blow out of shape with the slightest breeze, then use hair spray to hold it in place.

Men should also have two suits. Each should be two-piece and single-breasted with one and one half-inch cuffs on the pants. One suit should be navy blue and the other dark gray with a subtle, single, three-fourths inch gapped, white pin stripe. The stripe should be very discreet and only visible when you are within arm's length.

It's critical that you buy two suits for your job search. Then, you won't get stuck in a situation that can often occur. For example, the company representative with whom you are interviewing meets you at the airport (chances are you will travel by air for follow-up interviews) and you both go to dinner. You must wear the suit you wore while traveling. After wearing your suit all day and evening, the next day this suit is not acceptable in appearance for your interview. You need the second suit.

Your suits don't need to be extremely expensive, but they should be of good quality. There are several good brands, but one we consistently recommend is Hart, Schaffner & Marx. This company sells good quality, less expensive business suits and knows exactly what you need in a business cut. Sometimes, you can find two suits that are acceptable for interviews on sale for the price of one. Your suits should always be extremely well pressed for interviews.

Your shirts should be white with button-down collars. I usually suggest 100 percent cotton. Many business people who are constantly on the road have to send out their shirts to hotel laundries. Let me assure you that if you travel the circuit I travel, you won't be able to wear 99 percent of the shirts returned from these laundries. One side of the collar goes one way, the other another way. That's why you should wear shirts with button-down collars. Don't assume that the shirts you send to the laundry will be ironed satisfactorily. A typical scenario is that you get your laundry back at 7:00 P.M. Your interview is at 7:00 A.M. the next morning. You wear the shirt the way it is—or you don't wear it. You have no choice. The button-down design overcomes any collar problem caused by a laundry.

Your ties should be "power ties"—bold in color—so that they are the focal point. There's a very simple reason for this. When you travel, you can't take four or five suits with you and change your suit frequently. If you want to switch your tie in the middle of the day, 90 percent of those around you will think you've changed your entire suit.

You can't buy a $15 tie today that's acceptable for an interview. You will need to spend $30 or more. Don't ruin an interview for the sake of saving $10 or $15.

Wear good-quality socks that are over-the-calf, such as socks from Brooks Brothers. You can run in these socks, and they will stay up. Don't wear socks that bunch down around your ankles, as I so often see in interviews.

The shoe I recommend is a wine-colored, wing-tipped, lace-up or with a tassel cordovan. When you travel, you can't carry a lot of different shoes. You can wear the shoe I recommend with a tan, brown, black, or blue suit. It's an extremely acceptable shoe and is a good choice for interviews and casual wear. Be sure your shoes are well shined. There is no excuse for any other appearance. There are even small shoeshine kits available that you can carry in your pocket.

Occasionally, a recruiter will ask you to wear business casual attire for dinner or meetings other than the actual interview sessions. But what does that mean? There are many different definitions of business casual, especially now that more and more companies have instituted a business casual dress code in the office, either every day or on specific days, like Fridays or when there are no clients in the office. For men, I recommend quality slacks, a shirt, a tie, and a sport jacket. (A suit jacket worn with slacks is not a sport jacket.) Today, quality slacks and a long-sleeve, button-down collar pressed shirt without a tie and sport jacket is acceptable, but be careful. You can always remove a tie or jacket, but if the others with whom you are dining are wearing a tie and you are not, you will feel uncomfortable because of your lack of tie.

For women, I recommend a skirt and blouse with a blazer or a dress. Nice pant suits are acceptable for women today, but again, be careful. You want to portray a clean, crisp, professional look.

No matter what a recruiter suggests you wear for attire, I strongly encourage you to wear the upper end of what is permitted. After all, you are still in the interview process, even though it is not an interview for which you are dressing. Also, if you dress too casually, you are going to feel uncomfortable during the dinner or meeting and less confident. I promise you, you will not be successful feeling this way. Dress for confidence. Dress up rather than down. If you find your dinner companion isn't wearing a jacket or a tie, it's very simple to remove yours. **It's easy to dress down, but impossible to dress up.** Let me assure you that if you are in an interview and you're under-dressed, you can't make up the difference on the spot. Know ahead of time what will be expected of you. If the company with which you are interviewing does not advise you, ask what is appropriate to wear.

Remember that as a Development Candidate in the business world, you will be expected to lead, not follow. The way you dress and present yourself says a lot not only about you and your judgment but also about the company or product you will represent. Don't kid yourself. Companies want their employees to look professional and sharp. Today, companies want you to be comfortable, but no where in the plethora of definitions of "business casual" do the words "unprofessional" or "sloppy" appear.

Remember what you wear when you go to work for a company will be at your own discretion within their professional set of standards. You'll be measured primarily on your work performance, but in a job search, your clothes are a key factor that companies use to evaluate you and your judgment.

Glasses

Sunglasses should never be worn in an interview. Recruiters want to see your expression and make eye contact with you. It is very difficult, if not impossible, to see through tinted glasses. Some of you wear the photogrey glasses that change with sunlight. The unfortunate thing is that, many times, when you come into a hotel or any interview environment, you will sit next to a window. Photogrey will automatically tint the glass. These glasses are perfectly all right to work in under certain circumstances, but they are not the best for interviewing.

I also recommend that when you purchase glasses you choose professional frames that will be appropriate with the clothes you wear to your interviews. I do not recommend you wear military-issued glasses. The easiest way to be sure your selection is a good one is to try on the frames while wearing one of your business suits and standing in front of a full-length mirror.

Most importantly, have your glasses fitted properly (by a professional) so that you won't have to push your glasses into place repeatedly during the interview. Candidates often have developed such a habit of doing this that they make the motion of pushing their glasses into place even when they are not wearing them! Most optometrists will adjust your glasses while you wait free of charge. Therefore, take advantage of this service and make sure your glasses fit properly.

Being On Time

Few behaviors hinder your climb to the top of the corporate ladder more than being habitually late for commitments. When you are late in arriving for an event or appointment, in accomplishing an objective, in turning in a report, or in sending a thank-you note, the impression you leave is less than satisfactory. Make it a habit. Never be late.

I encourage you to look at being late for an interview from the point of view of a recruiter. Often, when you are late, you are thinking, "I'll only be a minute late—or, at the most, five minutes late." I encourage you to realize you are the only one who knows this. The person expecting you knows nothing. When you are late by even a minute, the recruiter is placed in the uncomfortable position of wondering where you are. Numerous possibilities present themselves—perhaps you are in the elevator, maybe you have forgotten the appointment, or perhaps you've even had an accident. As the minutes go by, the recruiter doesn't know whether to wait, make a phone call, or leave to do other work. In any case, your action has resulted in the recruiter wasting time. After you force a recruiter's anxiety level to climb, it may be difficult for you to have an objective interview.

Don't justify being late with excuses. They won't work. The point is this: Consider what being late says about you—nothing good! Being late to an interview, a meeting, an appointment—whatever it may be—implies that you do not care about the commitment enough to plan accordingly (this includes anticipating potential obstacles, like heavy traffic) and arrive on time.

I suggest that you always arrive at commitments five minutes before the scheduled time. Manage yourself and your surroundings such that you can easily meet your commitments. If you value something enough to commit to it, don't let something like being late destroy it for you.

What To Do And Not Do In The Interview
What are the most common things officers do and don't do in an interview? Probably the best learning experience an officer or any job candidate could have would be to sit in the corner of my

hotel room and observe others interview. Members of our team have come with me to military bases to watch as I conduct interviews throughout the course of the day. They each will tell you they were amazed at what they saw candidates do and not do.

Demeanor. Many officers come before recruiters as if they're carrying the weight of the world on their shoulders. We want someone who is relaxed, not afraid to smile, and eager to be there. Someone who has the ability to make the conversation flow. In a Development Candidate, we want to see a high level of poise and confidence. We expect maturity, and we expect you to be personable and able to interact easily with others. While we certainly understand you have some butterflies in your stomach, you want to show a lighter, more at ease, professional style. It is imperative that you contain your nervousness and demonstrate poise and confidence in an interview. Don't let poor demeanor rule you out.

Posture. Often, you must sit in chairs that contribute to poor posture. Sometimes, the armrests are positioned in a way that you cannot help but rest your elbows on them. When you do your hands are up in your face. I've seen people come in and talk through their hands, actually leaning on their hands at 9:00 A.M. as if they were tired.

Posture is important. Sit up straight in the chair. **Control your environment—don't let the environment control you.** You can change your posture. Don't sit there as stiff as a board. Be natural—but with good posture. And, it's okay to cross your legs. Don't sit on the front edge of your chair. Sit back in a professional, comfortable manner. When you want to show enthusiasm, lean forward slightly in your chair. Give yourself room for physical expressions, keeping in mind, of course, that your demeanor and presence must always be professional.

Chewing Gum. This is an automatic rule out. I'm always disappointed when an officer steps in front of me in an interview or at an Information Meeting attempting to communicate with me while chewing gum. It's rude and unprofessional. When I've declined officers for this reason and explained why, they are always quick to tell me they would never chew gum in front of a company. You've got to be kidding! Now, you're telling me you are simply selectively unprofessional! Please, never have anything in your mouth as you talk to others.

Smoking. Here's the rule on smoking—never, during an interview. Never. If you smoke, then smoke before you go to your breakfast, lunch, or dinner meeting, but do not smoke during an interview. When you're hired, it may be acceptable to smoke on the job or at least in designated smoking areas. However, more and more companies are hiring the non-smoker.

Foul Language. There can never be an excuse to use foul language in an interview, or, for that matter, anywhere in Corporate America. What you're saying is that you do not have the ability to express your point of view without it. If you do that, you're really telling Corporate America everything they want to know about you. There is absolutely no excuse for it. Every time a candidate has used foul language in an interview, I hear about it from the recruiter, and every time, they are declined by the recruiter. I always feel sorry for a person who uses foul language without thinking of the offending message it sends to others. Do yourself a favor and never bring foul language to an interview.

Nervous Habits. You should be able to come into an interview, regardless of the environment, and concentrate specifically on what you are doing. I've seen interviews take place in almost every location possible—hallways, parking lots, hotel rooms, or on a walk around the block.

Control the interviewing environment. Don't let nervous habits unconsciously make you look bad. Focus.

For example, in some hotels the room where the interview takes place has a window that looks out on the swimming pool. I've had candidates indicate they're more interested in checking out what's taking place at poolside than they are in focusing on the interview. If you're looking out the window at traffic on the street, you're losing vital concentration.

I've known recruiters who will purposely try to distract you. They may turn on the TV, without sound, to see if you can still focus on the interview rather than on the TV screen. If you don't have the ability to go into any environment and focus on the reason for being there, you won't accomplish your objective.

Many officers insist on fiddling with pens. There you are, during an interview—fiddling, as if it didn't mean anything, as if it didn't reveal an unconscious nervous habit. Another nervous habit is waving one leg back and forth when one leg is crossed over the other. I had one applicant who did this constantly, so I suddenly took my left arm and began waving it back and forth from my shoulder out. I continued to ask questions. The officer stared at me. I asked, "Am I bothering you?" He said, "Yes, you really are." I then pointed out his nervous habit, which had been distracting me. He sat very still for the balance of the interview and became conscious of a subconscious nervous habit.

You may say, "I would never do that." I have seen many people with nervous habits. The worst, unquestionably, is when people pop their knuckles. This is absolutely, positively obnoxious and rude. When I have brought these bad habits to their attention, they were not even conscious of them. So, this isn't something that just happens to a few people or the unfortunate few people. It happens to a lot of people. Be very careful of these negative unconscious habits.

Sometimes, I want to say to an officer I am interviewing, "Would you mind sitting on your hands?" Almost every second they're attempting to communicate with their hands. It's okay to do that on occasion. But, in the interview, you must do everything in moderation. You can't talk with your hands throughout an interview. It gets annoying—and we try to imagine you at a staff meeting or in a company presentation. It becomes so distracting that it's difficult to concentrate on what you're saying.

Many hotels have noisy air conditioning units. But, sometimes, officers will ignore the noise. They'll still talk in a normal tone of voice instead of lifting their voices to overcome the air conditioning. If I have to turn off the air conditioning in order to hear the officer, I'm going to decline him or her. If they're not aware enough to raise their voice over the noise, then they're really not the kind of person my companies are paying me to find.

Also, there's the problem of what some people do with their rings. I've had officers take off a wedding band and try it on each finger, not even aware of what they're doing. One man got his ring stuck on his thumb and had a hard time getting it off. Another put both little fingers in the wedding band. They got stuck, and I had to hold the wedding band in place, so this individual could pull his fingers out.

When a ring falls to the floor, it invariably rolls under the bed, under the couch, or under the table. It's embarrassing—you're sitting there in your good-looking two-piece suit. Then, suddenly, you're on the floor, trying to retrieve a ring from under your chair.

Watch your nervous habits. Don't stare out the window, gesture constantly with your hands, or fiddle with your wedding band. It's amazing how many people can be totally unaware of doing these things.

Smile. Remember to smile in the interview—a smile attracts a smile. A recruiter will never believe you are interested or excited about an opportunity if he or she never sees you smile during the interview. More importantly, how can you develop rapport with someone without smiling? You will be nervous in an interview but do not forget to smile. Smiling is an easy thing to do. It takes hardly any effort to form a smile, and the results can be profound in just about any situation. Try it today. Try it in an interview.

What To Take To An Interview
When you go to an interview, take a pen and spiral notebook that is small enough to fit in your suit coat pocket and nothing else. Make sure your pen is noise-proof and has no parts that click when you nervously hold it. You will use the notebook to take down an address (if a company wants you to send them something) or a phone number if the recruiter wants you to call him or her. You should pull out your notebook when you are introduced to some-one and write down the individual's name. I know how frequently you are introduced to people in the hiring and interview process, and this helps you remember.

If they are wearing a nametag, that is different. You can look at the nametag and have it remind you. Otherwise, do not be embarrassed about pulling the notebook out of your pocket and writing down the individual's name—particularly if you get into an interview where there are several recruiters. It's critical to write down their names to be able to remember them and to also send them thank-you letters later. Do not be afraid to ask them how to spell their names or to ask for clarification: "Tim? Or, did you say Jim?" There is absolutely nothing wrong with that. I know of many embarrassments where people have forgotten names. You shouldn't walk into the interview with the pad in your hand; it should be readily accessible. It should be clean so you don't have to thumb through pages finding a page to make a note on it. When you're through making notes on a particular company, remove the sheet from the notebook. Then, as you go into your next interview, you can again be prepared to write on a clean page.

The things you don't take with you into an interview are a tape-recorder, 3x5 note cards with questions on them, your laptop computer, or anything else that has no purpose.

I strongly recommend you go through careful self-evaluation after every interview. Interviewing is a skill and can be improved with examination and practice. See the interviewing self-evaluation exercise in Appendix C.

CHAPTER 5

Interviewing Strategy —
From Proving Your Fit To How To Close

*"**PCS** drove me to evaluate what I had done in the Air Force, why I did it, and what results I garnered. I gained insight into how I accomplished things and what set me apart from others. Now, as a recruiter, I look for this same insight in candidates—do they know what they have done? Do they know why they did it? What was their motivation? What was their plan of action? What were the results? It is questions like these that reveal what drives a person to success. Knowing the answers is what I have found invaluable to my own success."*
— Lisa A. M. Becker
Recruiting Representative
Guidant Corporation

CHAPTER 5

Interviewing Strategy —
From Proving Your Fit To How To Close

I want to introduce this chapter with some words of motivation. As I explained in the Foreword, there are three ways you can transition to the business world—you can either step up, step down or make a lateral move (step across) into a business career.

I've had officers (with whom Cameron-Brooks did not partner) call me after they have made the transition to the business world. They tell me they are disappointed with their career, that their leadership and interpersonal skills are not being utilized. Their military experience is not valued. They have less responsibility than when they were in the military. They are not on a track for management development. They tell me they worked hard and were successful in high school, in college, and in the military. They ask me, "Is there anything you can do to help me find a position where my skills are valued and where I will be on a track for upward mobility?" Unfortunately, there is nothing we can do for them. I empathize with them—what a waste of potential—but I do not sympathize. These officers clearly chose the easy way out of the military. Frequently, they tell me, "I had no choice—I did not have time to prepare. I was too busy in the military."

I say, "You did choose." We work every day to help our candidates work smart during their transition preparation. Until their final day in the military, our candidates are top performers. For months, sometimes even years before they exit the military, they engage in a rigorous transition preparation and development program while excelling in their military jobs. We work with them and help them to be smart workers. They have to produce on both fronts—in their military careers and in their transition preparation. Our candidates actually improve their performance in their military positions while they are enrolled in our development program because the concepts and skills they learn are applied in the workplace. Their marketability improves, and their military career improves, too! None of our candidates will tell you that preparing for a step up into a business career is easy. Choose to challenge yourself and work hard to be at your best for your interviews, and you will be able to compete for positions of enhanced responsibility and upward mobility. Choose the easy way out of the military and you will find a position below you. **If you want a world-class career, you need to do world-class preparation**.

Once you have committed to make a transition, this is the decision with which you are faced: Are you willing to leave the military for a career with less responsibility and opportunity? I wouldn't think so! A transition "up" is the only career move we are interested in facilitating. A transition up is where I want this book to take you. A transition up requires hours—hundreds of hours—of hard work, of self-examination, of research, of practice, but not everyone is willing to make a commitment of this degree. Transitioning up is not easy.

If you are still committed to stepping up into a business career and competing for development positions, stay with me. Dig into these next critical chapters. Concentrate. Think about what I am saying. Take notes. Get serious about what you need to do. You want to be at your "best" when you hit the marketplace.

Interviewing Fundamentals
At its most fundamental level, an interview is nothing more than a conversation that follows an agenda. From a recruiter's perspective,

the agenda is to make a determination at the end of the interview whether or not the candidate is a "fit." Your agenda (as the interviewee) is to prove that you are a fit with the opportunity.

When I ask most candidates what they think their agenda is in an interview, they often say things like, "My agenda is to determine if I want this job." While this may be a worthwhile objective for a follow-up interview, it has no place in an initial interview. After all, if you invest all your time in determining if you like the job, you waste precious time needed to convince the recruiter of your fit. At the end of the interview, you may come to the conclusion you really want the job, but the recruiter rules you out for obvious reasons (the recruiter owns the interview). **Your mission is to prove your fit**. You will have plenty of time after you get an offer to figure out if you prefer this job over another.

How do you prove your fit? You prove it on three fronts: ability, interest, and rapport. Communicating your fit is the most important strategy for successful interviewing. Make connecting on these three fronts your top priority throughout your interview.

Ability. Are you qualified to do this type of work? Do you have experiences that relate to the job/career for which you are interviewing? As a candidate you need to develop examples from your resume that demonstrate your ability to excel in a business career. Can you imagine hiring someone who was not qualified (could not do the job)? When you convey points of connection, the recruiter develops an understanding of your qualifications. This may seem obvious, but how do you communicate your ability to lead? How can you communicate initiative? How can you prove to a recruiter that you can solve complex problems? The only way to do this is to develop examples from your past that demonstrate your ability to do the job. Talk is cheap. Just saying that you can lead or assuming that just because you are a military officer companies will give you the benefit of the doubt doesn't work.

Interest. Imagine you are interviewing a very qualified person for an important job who does not seem genuinely interested in working with you. What conclusion would you come to regarding his or her fit? A big part of proving your fit is showing interest in the opportunity. You could be completely qualified for a job from an ability perspective and still fail in the interview. A frequent reason for this is that the candidate does not prove he or she is interested. Proving you are interested in an opportunity does not simply mean saying the words, "I'm interested." Much more importantly, it means doing your homework before the interview, developing a good understanding of the business world, asking good questions, showing curiosity, etc. When you do this, the recruiter sees that you have strong interest in the company and the position. You can perform the first step perfectly, but, if the recruiter does not fully understand your interest, you will not succeed in an interview.

Rapport. Now imagine that you are interviewing a perfectly qualified person who also has good reasons why he or she is interested. However, throughout the interview you just don't have a good feeling about the candidate as a person. You can't connect with this person. You're having trouble imagining him or her working beside you. You're not sure how this individual will fit in "culturally" with your company. What conclusion would you come to as a recruiter? I can tell you 100 percent of corporate recruiters will decline a candidate whom they do not think is a good interpersonal fit. This is a very common reason for candidates to fail. If you don't believe me, ask yourself why so many people with great credentials have so much trouble finding great jobs. Generally speaking, this third step gives many military officers great difficulty. Since most people don't do enough preparation for interviews, they are nervous throughout the interview, hurting their rapport-building skills. In some cases your military training hurts you. Most military officers are not comfortable using first names, a key part of building rapport in the business world. The military uses employment contracts, diminishing the need for personally connecting with the people in your office or unit. Again, this kind of behavior is completely foreign to most businesses. Rapport-building skills are not something you can just wing in an interview. By diligently preparing for an interview and focusing on interpersonal skills, it will be much easier to build rapport with recruiters throughout an interview. It takes practice.

Proving your ability and interest and developing rapport are fundamental to interviewing success. All three have equal weight in the eyes of corporate recruiters. As you prepare for corporate interviews, evaluate all of your interview answers on how they add value on all three fronts of proving fit.

Types Of Interviews
Basically, there are three types of interviews:

1) **Traditional** (the recruiter works off a list of prepared questions);
2) **Resume** (the recruiter works off your resume asking questions about your jobs/accomplishments); and
3) **Conversational** (the recruiter asks no formal questions but rather exchanges information in an unstructured and conversational manner).

For many officers the conversational interview is the most difficult. Candidates have remarked to me that they were surprised the recruiters spent 20 to 30 minutes in conversation before the interview actually began. Do not mistake a conversational interview. Just because recruiters do not ask a lot of questions does not mean they do not expect a lot from you in the interview. They are in fact interviewing you! All interviews are about connecting, and the conversational interview is no different. You will be evaluated from the moment you enter the room. By listening carefully during a conversational interview, you will find that it is easy to identify times you can professionally interject points of connection to prove your fit on the three fronts. Practice the conversational interview with a study partner or your spouse/ significant other. The key is to practice, practice, practice!

Time To Verbalize

Military officers have a phenomenon in their backgrounds of "moving to the next step based on the observation of past performance."

You go to grade school. Your teachers observe you. At the end of that observation period, they grade you. Based upon those grades, you take the next step and move on to junior high. Based on observation and grades, you then move on to high school. The procedure follows you into college, then into ROTC or an academy, and then into the military.

You are observed and graded. You then take the next logical step. However, when you leave the military and make the decision to go into business, you must verbalize these past successes. You're not afforded the opportunity to be observed before being graded— the observation is based on how you verbalize your successes in an interview. No other point makes more officers fail in the interview process. You have never had to verbalize past accomplishments, your leadership style, or how you solve problems. You haven't practiced doing so.

It's time to start practicing because in the interview you are expected to verbalize your successes. No one else and nothing else can do it for you. You will fail in your interviews if you cannot verbalize your past performance effectively. It doesn't matter that Roger Cameron says you have a solid background of achievements or that you have written records of great performance (very few recruiters want to read your military evaluations), you need to be able to verbalize that performance.

Consider Your Audience

To communicate effectively with corporate recruiters, you must rid your vocabulary of military terms and acronyms. You cannot communicate effectively in the business world using terms such as MQ office, platoon, unit, battalion, TDY, NTC, down range, Gleem analysis, etc. If you would like to test me, go to any street corner in America, stop the first 10 people and ask them some questions: "What is the difference between a platoon and a company? A unit and a battalion? What is TDY?"

In the military you understand these terms. But in a corporate interview, your audience is not the military. Even if recruiters have a background in or are familiar with the military, they expect you to communicate in their language. After all, the purpose of the interview is to gain a position in the business world. In a corporate interview, why would you be talking in any language other than theirs?

Once I was conducting a workshop in Pensacola, Florida, and an hour and a half into the two-hour workshop I said, "Enough. I am going to conclude this workshop unless everyone here agrees to something. Tomorrow morning I want everyone to get up early, buy *The Wall Street Journal*, and read every single article until you are positive you understand the language Corporate America speaks. Then call me and tell me what it is." If you don't know what Corporate America's language is, do this exercise yourself. **Corporate America talks in numbers.** Take any article from *The Wall Street Journal*, remove the numbers, and I challenge you to make sense of the article. Learn "corporate speak" if you want successful interviews.

You might think this is a minor issue, but take a moment and listen to the conversations around you in the military. How often are military terms and acronyms thrown into a sentence? A lot. Most officers do not even realize that to most of us, you are speaking a foreign language when you use military terms. It is ingrained. It is time to break this habit and express yourself using language a corporate recruiter will understand.

Learn About The Business World
You cannot be successful in a corporate interview without having an understanding of the world in which you are pursuing a career.

A recruiter is going to be suspicious of your interest in having a business career if you cannot talk intelligently about business. Recruiters want to believe that although you have been successful in the military, you are prepared for the adjustment to the business world and that you will function successfully in this environment. They also want to see that you are excited about a career in business.

Educating yourself about the business world will enable you to make connections between your military background and the business world. You must be able to connect your background and skills to the position for which you are interviewing and demonstrate to the recruiter that you have the ability to do the job.

If you haven't already, make business reading a daily habit. The best way to learn about the business world while you are in the military is through a quality business reading program. See Appendix B for sources I recommend for increasing your knowledge about the business world.

Why Corporate America Hires The Military Officer
Companies hire the JMO for three major reasons. Think about

these reasons as you prepare for corporate interviews. Be a smart salesperson: **give recruiters what they want!**

Leadership. The military officer brings the business world both subordinate and "up" leadership experience. Subordinate leadership means that you have full responsibility and full authority. Up leadership means that you have full responsibility and no authority. The latter is found most often in staff positions. If you are a program manager, you have full responsibility to drive the program to a successful conclusion, but you have no authority over the contractors doing the job. Corporate America likes your ability to lead in both of these situations.

Accomplishments. You bring the business world a track record of "real-world" accomplishments. Real-world means bringing important objectives to fruition against time, money, assets, quality and a major mission. This is difficult if not impossible to find on the college campus.

Objective and Subjective Skill Development. You bring us an enhanced skill set. You have honed your ability to solve problems, to handle multiple objectives simultaneously, to work effectively in a wide variety of circumstances and with people of diverse backgrounds. You are more action-oriented. You are more goal-oriented. You have learned to do more with less.

Know the driving forces behind Corporate America believing in you. You must touch on these factors in your answers and show the recruiter you have what he or she wants. What value would an answer have if it didn't lend credence to the main reasons a recruiter wants to hire you?

Spontaneous And Reflective Questions
Recruiters ask two types of questions in an interview: spontaneous and reflective. Spontaneous questions take about five percent of

any interview. Examples include the following: How do you pronounce your last name? Where did you go to college? What was your grade point average? What was your major? Where is your hometown? Obviously, these answers are on the tip of your tongue, and you can quickly, spontaneously answer them.

The most significant and frequently asked question in an interview is the reflective question. This type of question requires more thought than spontaneous questions. Examples are: What is your leadership style? How do you solve complex problems? What motivates you? Give me an example of an accomplishment. Give me an example of a failure. **Your answers to reflective questions are key to securing a recruiter's interest.**

Talking About Accomplishments
The most common reflective question asked in an interview is, "Give me an example of a significant accomplishment. Why was it significant, and how did you accomplish it?" Accomplishment questions are the most important questions you will get in an interview because they provide proof of the level of contribution you made to your past organizations. Remember, Corporate America likes people who have a track record of making things happen. In other words, the more accomplishments you have, the stronger your track record. Prepare multiple (10) examples of accomplishments in all of your military jobs as well as at least two from high school and two from college.

What is an accomplishment? An accomplishment is the attainment of a goal—a time when you set a high, demanding goal and motivated a group of people to make it happen. The best accomplishment examples should come from your work experience where you took the initiative to find better ways to get results. Doing your daily job is not an accomplishment. Working hard by putting in 18-hour days is not an accomplishment. Developing a new maintenance process that improved combat readiness is an accomplishment. Developing a new training program that set a record at the National Training Center is an accomplishment. Creating an improved budget tracking and approval system that reduced processing time is an accomplishment. The key is to have process-oriented accomplishments that show you can look critically at a process and champion a cause on how to do it better.

A good accomplishment should have four key parts:

1) **The accomplishment sentence.** You should state your accomplishment in one succinct sentence. For example, "I developed a new vehicle inspection program that reduced vehicle downtime by 25 percent and improved combat readiness." The vehicle inspection program is the accomplishment (a new way of doing things), and the reduced downtime and improved combat readiness is proof that the new inspection program made an impact. Remember, it is critical that your accomplishments show impact and bottom-line results (improved capability to do your mission). Deliver your accomplishment with passion and excitement. It's very hard to excite someone else about your accomplishment if you don't sound excited.

2) **Significance.** Because most recruiters know very little about the military, you will need to articulate the importance of your accomplishments. In other words, why is vehicle maintenance important, and how does it impact on combat readiness? I encourage you to explain the big picture significance of your accomplishment (think like a general or admiral). Remember, you must show how the accomplishment had a bottom-line impact on the primary mission of the Armed Forces (combat readiness). When possible, you should quantify the significance of your accomplishment. Verbally, create a picture using numbers and dollars to get a recruiter's attention and interest. You should also explain the difficulty factor in your accomplishment. Your issue

takes on more importance and significance when you have a high difficulty factor. Maybe you had less than normal time, dollars, people, training, etc.

3) **Thought process.** How did you think through the accomplishment? In other words, what research or analysis did you do to frame the issues in the accomplishment? Did you look at historical records, did you collaborate with experts, or did you flowchart a process looking for bottlenecks? What conclusions did you draw from your research? What were the top two or three key issues relating to the success of your accomplishment? Did it have to do with training or reengineering a process? Bottom line, you need to be able to impress a recruiter that you can dig into a problem, understand cause and effect, and draw conclusions that map out the issues relating to the success of an accomplishment.

4) **Action.** This is where you show the steps you took to accomplish your objective. In step three you show that you can think through a problem, and in step four you show you can make it happen. For instance, you determine in step three that a key issue is inadequate individual training. In step four you discuss the training program you developed as a solution to the inadequate training. Be careful; don't let the recruiter think your solution to a key issue is simply a Band-Aid (short-term approach). Development leaders put long-term solutions in place as opposed to quick fixes. Also, in this step it is critical for you to show ownership of actions by using the pronoun "I." The more ownership statements you make, the greater demonstration of your role in making it happen. Finally, wrap your last statement back into the accomplishment (step one) to make a clean closure on your answer.

This is a framework that you can apply to all of your significant accomplishment answers. The more comfortable you become with the framework, the easier it will be for you to develop and deliver multiple accomplishment examples. Remember, these examples are critical to establishing your track record of making a significant impact throughout your military (as well as high school and college) career. I promise you, evidence of a strong track record will significantly improve your ability to step up into a new business career.

Competency-Based Interview

The competency-based interview is a popular interviewing strategy for determining your ability to perform. It is being used more and more and is highly effective. The goal of the interview is to uncover your behavioral traits—those skills or characteristics that you apply consciously or unconsciously to accomplish objectives.

Examples of questions recruiters will ask in the competency-based interview are open-ended questions that typically begin with "Tell me about," such as, "Tell me about a time you read a book to learn a new skill and applied the concepts you learned to improve a process at work" or "Tell me about a time you were thrown into a new job and achieved results by analyzing the situation and establishing priorities." Competency-based interview questions also can be "how" questions, such as, "How do you build a team?" or "How do you build relationships with difficult people?" Recruiters want to hear stories about accomplishments and in those stories they look for evidence of competencies. They then compare those competencies with the specific traits they require in future leaders for their company.

What is a competency or behavioral trait? It is a **consistently** demonstrated characteristic. The competencies companies look for in Development Candidates are determined by analyzing the characteristics of top management. They want Development Candidates with similar characteristics. If you were interviewing for a non-development position, the competencies would be based on the job and what it takes to perform in that specific position.

Many companies will require some of the same competencies. For example, almost every company wants people who are positive thinkers, results-oriented, team players, effective communicators, etc. Companies differ on how they prioritize competencies. Some place emphasis on creativity, while others value drive or competitiveness.

Competencies must be demonstrated in your answers; they cannot be stated. A competency is a consistently demonstrated characteristic. Your competencies will show up again and again in your answers to a recruiter's questions. For example, if one of your competencies is initiative, evidence of you having initiative should show up in your answers again and again. The key here is that unless that trait shows up in multiple examples, it will not be considered a competency or demonstrated behavioral trait.

It's taboo for you to actually state the trait. You can't say, for example, that you're "intelligent and competitive." You must illustrate these characteristics by discussing your past accomplishments.

It's critical that you take ownership of your competencies by using the pronoun "I" in your answers. Do not use the pronoun "you" or "we" in your answers. Recruiters want to know about you and what your competencies are—not those of a hypothetical person or of your team.

To prepare for this type of interview, start by analyzing exactly **how you** accomplish difficult objectives. This isn't a five-minute job. I envision it taking you a full day—or longer. As you examine past accomplishments, make a list of those **common** behavioral traits that appear in situation after situation. Note how some traits are automatic, or subconscious, and how others require a conscious effort on your part.

List the traits (or characteristics) that appear frequently and that result in outstanding performance. This is a key point. The trait should be developed to a level that results in exceptional achievement; otherwise, the list is meaningless to you. We all organize, manage our time, and interact with others, but do we do it to the degree that we would be considered outstanding in the trait?

Next, I would suggest you prioritize your list of traits and keep them firmly in mind with examples of accomplishments. The end result is that you'll be armed with the information about your most outstanding behavioral traits, and you will be able to give the recruiter concise, articulate descriptions of them.

Here's an exercise you can try that will help you identify the noteworthy traits you possess: Lean back in your chair, close your eyes, and visualize an individual who has worked for or with you and whose performance was outstanding. Think about what you most admired about that individual's performance. When I ask candidates to do this in interview workshops, they consistently mention the same characteristics. The individual they describe is always a hard worker, has a positive attitude, is goal-oriented, is a team player, etc. Now, think about the traits you have identified and which of those you think describe you. Think about situations that have occurred in which you have used these traits and accomplished your goals. Use the tape recorder to record your answer.

Appendix A contains a list of key competencies. Use this list to help you identify those characteristics you think best describe your demonstrated behavioral traits or strengths.

Some examples of the characteristics recruiters want to see in your answers are:
- Competitiveness;
- Creativity;
- Effective, persuasive communication;
- Effective use of time;
- Goal-oriented;
- Innovative;
- Make-it-happen attitude;
- Organizational ability;
- Pre-problem solution ability;
- Prioritization ability;
- Sense of urgency;
- Strong work ethic;
- Success-driven;
- Successful interaction with peers, superiors, and team members;
- Team player; and
- Technical aptitude.

High Energy Level

Companies say to us, "Don't bring me candidates who are tired. We want people with high energy." To them high energy means the ability of an individual to put out as much work in the eighth hour of the day as he or she does in the first hour. After all, people are paid as much for the last hour as for the first hour.

In an interview we measure high energy in three ways:

1) **Visible high energy—how you walk.** Do you demonstrate a sense of urgency? A favorite recruiter of mine at Texas Instruments likes to stand outside his door about five minutes before the time of an interview so that he can see candidates turn the corner down the hall. If they don't pick up their pace between the back of the hall and his door, they are on the downhill side before stepping into the interview. Recruiters want to see that you have

energy in the way you walk. Keep in mind that you may be observed outside the office where you are interviewed. Maintain a lively pace no matter where you are.

2) **Feeling of high energy—handshake.** When you shake hands, it should be purposeful. You should step into the handshake, whether it's with a man or a woman. The handshake should be firm—full into the hand, showing a physical demonstration of high energy rather than strength. Energy should flow from you to the person with whom you're shaking hands.

3) **Audible high energy—enthusiasm in your voice.** Recruiters want to hear the energy in your voice. Does your voice convey (with changes in its tone and pitch) excitement and eagerness for the work?

I remember listening to a professor of military science talk to an ROTC group at a major southern college. He had a strong voice, but he turned his audience off about five minutes into his speech. They were looking at the floor, out the windows, and at their books and papers. At first, I couldn't understand why his audience was paying so little attention to him. Then, I realized he had absolutely no voice inflection. His voice was booming, but everything came out in a monotone. He didn't modulate his voice.

Voice inflection and verbal enthusiasm go hand in hand. Too often, companies say to me, "Roger, they said the correct things but not in a convincing manner." If you communicate with enthusiasm—with passion—recruiters are more likely to believe you.

Delivering Your Answers. How you say your answers is important. Use the following exercises to critique your articulation and speech patterns.

Exercise #1

Prepare an answer to the interview question, "Tell me about yourself." This is a very common interview request. You need to explain or present your background (high school, college, and military achievements) to an interviewer in a clear and concise manner. An interview is a **conversation** with the interviewer. Therefore, be very careful not to come across as though you are giving a canned answer or speech. Your discussion about yourself should be sincere and natural.

Have your spouse/significant other or a friend listen to your answer—or record it on a tape recorder. Concentrate on speaking clearly and enunciating your words. Be aware of your voice projection and yet be sensitive to your impact on the other person.

- Are you speaking too loudly or too softly?
- Do you drop the volume of your voice at the end of sentences?
- Do you talk too quickly?
- Do you slur your words together?
- Do you talk more slowly than is normal for a conversation?
- Are you picking your words too carefully?
- How fluid is your delivery?

Have the other person critique you, and, if you have used a tape recorder, critique yourself.

Exercise #2

Prepare a speech on a subject of importance to you. Present this speech to your spouse/significant other or a friend and record it on tape. The purpose of this exercise is to reveal to you how your speaking pattern varies when you give a speech versus when you are carrying on a conversation. In an interview it is very important for you to be conversational, natural, and sincere. **You should not sound like you are giving a speech**.

Listen to the tape recording of your speech. Compare it to the tape of your reply in Exercise #1. You should notice the differences in your speaking patterns. Do not fall into "giving a speech" in an interview.

Making Things Happen
One of the major points you want to convey in an interview is that you are a make-it-happen, goal-oriented, success-driven person. Think of times you accomplished tough objectives. What were the obstacles you had to overcome? It's not enough to simply tell the recruiter you are a make-it-happen type of person, you must **show** the recruiter that you are by giving the recruiter **proof and evidence** of your ability to make things happen.

I was in Colorado Springs speaking with an Air Force officer whom I had just declined. I asked the young man if there were any insight or help I could give him. He said, "Mr. Cameron, could you tell me in one sentence what it is that recruiters are looking for most in a Development Candidate?" It almost made me think I had made a mistake in declining him. I replied that recruiters are simply looking for an individual who can make things happen—someone who is goal-oriented and success-driven.

Corporations don't want to hire people who rationalize failures with excuse after excuse. Typical excuses include the following: "Oh, I'm sorry I'm late. I didn't know it was going to rain." "I didn't know Sally was going to take off for four weeks of vacation." "I didn't know the parts were going to come in late." "I didn't know my car was going to have a flat tire." "I didn't know." Too many people feel that as long as they have an excuse it is all right to fail. Recruiters and managers disagree. They are looking for people who find solutions to problems and make them successes; individuals who have the desire and ability to overcome adversity and see goals to completion.

Look around you in the military. I'm sure you know people who have a tremendous ability to get things done. You call them "go-to" people. Those individuals are mission-oriented and the kind of people we want to hire. When you come to Corporate America, many times you will be faced with difficult objectives. There are people who throw up their hands and quit when the going gets difficult. This is not the kind of person who is considered a Development Candidate going to the top of a major corporation. The best compliment I can hear is, "He or she is a make-it-happen type of person."

Certain people have the ability to do it, and others don't. It's one of the reasons we have to interview as many people as we do in a year to find the candidates we want. It's like the individual who interviews with me and has five officer evaluations—all average. Interestingly enough, none of them were her fault! In each case, she was a victim of circumstance. We may think this can happen on occasion. But, if every rater, perhaps five different ones, come up with the same conclusion—there's little doubt as to what our decision is going to be in this situation.

I remember a young man in El Paso, Texas, who had an appointment with me at 6:00 P.M. He arrived at the door 15 minutes late. As I went to the door, he said, "I'm sorry I'm late; the traffic was bad." It was obvious to me this individual thought nothing of being late because he had an excuse. I really don't know of any place, including Fredericksburg, Texas, where the traffic isn't bad at 6:00 P.M. Unfortunately, he never recovered from his downhill start with me. If the person was really intent on accomplishing an objective, he would have left early to compensate for heavy traffic.

Are you a make-it-happen type of person? We want to be able to give you tough objectives and know without a doubt that you will bring it back to us successfully completed.

Making Eye Contact

It's critical in developing rapport with a recruiter that you make eye contact as you respond to his or her questions. Have confidence in your answers. Show that confidence by looking the recruiter directly in the eye.

Often, interviewees lose eye contact when it's most important—with a difficult question that may be uncomfortable to answer. That's when I see eyes go to the floor, the ceiling, the window. You simply cannot do this.

Have you noticed that people "talk" with their eyes? Eyes can sparkle, look bland, or look suspicious. Don't you find you often make judgments based upon what you see in someone's eyes? Don't you question when someone doesn't look you in the eye? You may think, "Are they uninterested, bored, uncaring, or lacking in self-confidence?" Your eyes should show interest, enthusiasm, understanding, curiosity, warmth, and feeling.

Be aware of your eye contact. Where do you look when you talk to someone? Do you look at their mouth or do you look them in the eye? If you are not accustomed to having direct eye contact, it can be awkward at first, but, if you concentrate and practice, you will become comfortable with it. Eye contact should be natural, so do not "stare people down." Glance away only about 10 percent of the time.

With good eye contact, you will appear more confident and self-assured. People will listen to you and actually hear more of what you say. Almost all of us can improve our eye contact, so make yourself conscious of yours and work to make it better. I promise you, it will improve your chances for interview success.

Enthusiasm

We love to see individuals who are excited to get out of bed in the morning—excited about doing whatever they have to do. It doesn't make any difference whether we're picking somebody to play bridge, throw horseshoes, play basketball, or hire as an employee. We like people who have a sparkle in their eyes and a smile on their face. They can laugh at themselves. They create a positive, pleasant, professional aura about themselves.

I have seen enthusiastic people have great success at interviewing. Other people with even better credentials have not done as well because they simply didn't have that sparkle in their eye. I've seen enthusiasm outweigh some negatives in the interview. Recruiters say, "Roger, there are some things I don't like about this candidate, but I have to tell you something. She is so enthusiastic and upbeat. She is someone I would want to work for us. I have absolutely no doubt we can work through the couple of things in her background that could have been better." When you go into an interview, don't leave the enthusiasm at home whether the interview is with Roger Cameron or a corporate recruiter. We're all the same. We love to see enthusiastic individuals.

I have witnessed some candidates attempt to get by only on their enthusiasm. I am here to tell you that will never happen. No quality company will hire any officer with only one strong stave in the barrel. Enthusiasm in itself will not get you a job, but it can iron out a few wrinkles that a recruiter might see in your background.

Testing Conviction—The Negative Interview

The negative interview is designed to test your conviction about career objectives. Companies feel that if they can talk you out of what you want to do, they have proven you have less conviction. For a manufacturing position, recruiters might ask the question,

"What is your opinion of shift work?" Their purpose in asking is that we have had people leave manufacturing in Corporate America because they didn't like shift work. It's pretty hard to go into an interview and say, "I'm really excited about shift work." But, one of your early promotion levels in manufacturing may be to manage a 24-hour operation. Each shift is unique and has its own idiosyncrasies regarding how you interact and motivate team members to perform. If you know one of your early lines of promotion is to manage a 24-hour operation, then, obviously, it would be better to have experienced yourself each of the different shifts during the 24 hours. Many of you coming out of the military have not been able to get your master's degree because of TDY assignments, down range work in the field, deployment, etc. Sometimes, you can get a better quality MBA during daytime hours than in the evening. Shift work early in your career can be an ideal way for you to work toward a master-level degree.

When recruiters attempt to talk you out of a job, they may use different tactics such as, "Well, you're an outstanding candidate, and I really feel our company should hire you. However, I feel you would be better suited for position A than the position for which you are interviewing." Often, they're simply testing your ability to be committed to and convinced about the position for which you are interviewing. This is what we call the negative interview. For instance, if you are applying for a sales position, they might say, "Sales—I think you have strong poise and self-confidence, but you have to understand, with sales you're going to get a lot of negative aspects within a day. For example, prospective customers may be slamming the door in your face or canceling an appointment at the last minute (when you're already in your car driving there). You're going to end up wasting some time in a day. It's very difficult for you to organize and manage your time effectively. However, I believe you have the ability to handle other positions in our company that are equally outstanding. Would you like me to refer your resume to other departments?"

Again, they may simply be attempting to determine your conviction. Be careful!

A couple of companies in the follow-up interview process have a designated negative interviewer whose sole purpose is to try to talk you out of the job you're seeking. Unfortunately, not all candidates have listened to me, and they have allowed a company to talk them out of the job. I've actually had candidates come back to me and say, "Roger, I remember what you said, but I'm confident that's not what the company was doing. They actually thought I was better for something else." I moaned! Then, true enough, the candidate was declined for lack of conviction. As a military officer, you're coming out three to eight plus years behind your age group. If you're going to enter the race at that point, you must be committed. You must have conviction. You must know what you want. You must be able to focus and concentrate on that objective. Don't let somebody sway you 30 seconds into an interview.

Occasionally, the negative interview is used to determine poise and self-confidence. Sometimes, recruiters use it "to push on the end of your nose" to see what reaction they will get. While this is rarely used in interviewing today, at the very least I want to make you aware of it. Normally, the type of negative questions you will hear are, "A 3.5 grade point average—why wasn't it better?" Notice, it's a negative question on a positive point, which is usually the case. In other words, it isn't for the purpose of embarrassing you. It is for the purpose of determining how you handle a negative situation. In Corporate America, just as in the military, you will not always be in a positive situation. At times you'll need to deal with difficult issues. We want to see if you have gained the skill and maturity in the military to be able to do so. We want to see you handle negative situations positively. Do your neck and ears turn red? Do you put on the boxing gloves? Or, do you simply square the shoulders, look the recruiter in the eye, and handle it positively? It will potentially come up in interviews. Always remember that the objective is not to embarrass but to determine poise and self-confidence.

Bottom line: Never, never be negative or combative with a recruiter. Avoid using the word "no" in your answers. For example, in answering the question, "A 3.5 grade point average—why wasn't it better?" agree with the recruiter. Most candidates immediately want to take the recruiter to task on this grade point average—after all, a 3.5 GPA is better than average. I recommend you begin your response with the word, "yes." "Yes, I recognize a 3.5 GPA is not perfect. I worked very hard for my grades and am confident if all I had had to do in college were academics, I would have done better. I stretched myself to the limit between ROTC and other extracurricular activities, and, though through it all I gained valuable time management skills, my GPA was slightly compromised." Deliver your answer without rancor in your voice. Show maturity. Be professional. Never be combative. Recruiters and company managers want to hire individuals who know how to handle negative situations in a positive manner.

Two Or More Recruiters
Frequently, two or more recruiters will interview you. Sometimes only one recruiter will actually participate in the interview. Before the interview, determine if all of the recruiters will participate in the interview. If a recruiter is placed out of your sight, don't include him or her in the interview. Simply greet all of the recruiters at the beginning of the interview and afterwards. Be sure to remember the names of all recruiters present for the interview.

If more than one recruiter interviews you, maintain eye contact with each one when you deliver your answers. Give the recruiter who asks the question the initial and final eye contact. For example, let's say Recruiter A asks you a question. Begin your answer with eye contact with that recruiter. Continue your answer and pick up eye contact with Recruiter B, C, etc. Conclude your answer with eye contact with Recruiter A. If the question is substantive and requires a lengthy answer, you may change eye contact several times, always ending by giving eye contact with the recruiter who asked the question.

Treat each recruiter with an equal amount of attention and respect, regardless of the recruiter's age or gender. I have seen some candidates pay more attention to the male recruiters even when they have been told that the female recruiter had more hiring influence. Don't let this happen to you. Obviously, it will rule you out.

Always remember: companies are looking for young men and women who have poise and self-confidence. These qualities are important to portray in one-on-one situations as well as group meetings.

Closing The Interview
There are two types of "closes" in an interview. One is an informal close, which you do throughout the interview. The other is a formal close and occurs at the conclusion of the interview. It is critical in an interview that you do both.

The informal close is simply a matter of making points of connection. Throughout the interview give the recruiter concrete evidence of your ability to succeed in the position, of your strong interest in the opportunity, and of your interpersonal fit. Help the recruiter "see" your fit on all three fronts.

The formal close occurs at the end of the interview. The most common signal that the interview is nearing its end is when the recruiter looks at you and asks if you have any questions. This is when you should ask one or two quality questions you prepared specifically for the interview or questions that came to mind during the interview. Remember—they must be quality questions. This is one of the last impressions you will leave with the recruiter. You want it to be positive.

If you have already had a chance to ask questions, you can go back to an issue discussed earlier in the interview if you feel it can make a positive influence on the outcome of the interview. Let's say you did not feel one of your responses was adequate or you missed an opportunity to give information that is important to your job pursuit. Go back and restate your attitude and provide the information now. Make sure it is a positive restatement or addition to the interview. Again, you want to end on a positive note, not a negative one. Be smart.

How do you close the interview? The closing should be a natural exchange—as natural as thanking someone for taking you to dinner or sharing advice with you. In the case of a corporate interview, **you close by letting the recruiter know of your sincere interest in the opportunity and why.**

This is the last statement you want to leave in the recruiter's mind as you exit the interview. It should be positive and unique to that company—not the job! Or, if you choose to close on the job, it should always be after expressing interest in the company. The company is permanent; the job is temporary. If your interview goes the full time, you may have only seconds to deliver a close. You should think about and prepare your "close" before entering the interview. Again, it must be a statement that is company-specific. If your close can be said to more than one company, it will do you more harm than good.

Close the interview by being upbeat. Candidates sometimes walk away from interviews in which they have a high degree of interest without expressing their interest. If you are truly interested in the company and in the position, you cannot afford to leave the interview without letting the recruiter know this.

Typically people are attracted to companies because they like the company philosophy, high quality products, market share, sales growth, unique customers, or market, etc. When you share with a recruiter the issues that excite you about the opportunity, back up the issues with detail, i.e., what philosophy, what products, what market share, what sales growth, what unique customer, etc., and support your statements with why these issues are exciting to you. Make your comments specific. Close with enthusiasm and believability.

Bottom line: do not leave the interview without telling the recruiter you are interested in the opportunity!

If you do not have a strong interest in the opportunity, do not tell the recruiter you do. There are going to be times when you interview with a high quality company that for one reason or another just does not fit with your career goals at the time. You should not mislead the recruiter by overstating your interest. Be careful not to close any doors, however. It sometimes is necessary to conduct follow-up interviews (which allow you to meet other people who work for the company, see the working environment, the location, etc.) before you can determine your interest in a company. Don't rule yourself out by prematurely reserving interest in a company.

We've talked a lot about interviewing strategy and what needs to happen in an interview for you to be successful. Let's turn now, keeping our interviewing strategy and tips in mind, to how to handle and develop the best answers to the "big" questions recruiters will ask you in a corporate interview.

CHAPTER 6

Facing The Big Questions —
Developing The Best Answers

"Since leaving the military, I have had great success in the corporate world and I attribute much of this success to the knowledge I gained from PCS. It will teach you how Corporate America works and what it takes to be successful in business. All of Roger's insight and advice are backed up with thousands of successful career transitions. Even today, four years after leaving the military, I still use the knowledge I learned from PCS. My military experience is an important part of who I am and why I am successful. Roger taught me to believe this and how to use it to my advantage. I don't worry about questions about my military experience anymore—I thrive on them."
— Stephen P. Burke
Staff Field Sales Engineer
Cypress Semiconductor

CHAPTER 6 ⸻⸻⸻⸻

Facing The Big Questions —
Developing The Best Answers

Understanding The Big Questions
To deliver the best answers to the significant questions asked in an interview, let's first understand two basic philosophies, which are the basis for 90 percent of the questions you will be asked.

One philosophy behind a recruiter's questions is to determine the quality or difficulty factor of your successes. How is success judged? By the accomplishment of an objective. We all judge success similarly. What makes us unique are our objectives. How do you judge the quality of a success? Obviously, not every success is of equal quality. Consequently, we judge the quality of success by the difficulty factor. The greater the difficulty, the greater the significance of the accomplishment. You must realize that if success is the accomplishment of an objective, the flip side of the coin is that failure is the non-accomplishment of an objective. You can have a slight failure or a catastrophic failure. You can have a slight success, or you can have a phenomenal success. Recruiters want to know the quality or difficulty factor of your accomplishments. Verbalize your successes in such a way that the recruiter can determine the degree of success or the degree of failure.

The other philosophy on which a recruiter bases questions is to discover how you perform—how you get things done. Companies want people who think outside of the box, who know what needs to be done, who see what can be improved and who have the leadership skills, initiative, and track record for working with others to get it done. Corporate America will not hire process performers. We want leaders—people who will forge new tracks. The business world is ferociously competitive and extremely dynamic. To be successful today, companies must be reactive as much as they are proactive.

Frequently, recruiters ask the question, "If you take all of the assets you have and use on a daily basis, which ones do you feel you can improve upon?" The key word is can. The attitude we're looking for in candidates is a **drive for excellence**, a belief that they can improve what they're doing and that they hope to be able to do so even at age 98. You can give an excellent speech, but you can give an even better speech. You can have a great command, but you can have an even better command. You can run a four-minute mile, but you can run an even faster mile. We look for people with great attitudes about improving and pushing themselves.

Recruiters will ask the question: "Which one of your assets do you feel you need to improve?" This can be a difficult question. Need, by definition, means that you have a significant weakness in that area. I can't imagine Dell Computer Corporation, Motorola, Arthur Andersen, Ericsson or any other great company coming to me and saying, "Roger, travel around the world, and let us pay you a fee to hire an individual who has weaknesses." Be careful to distinguish between the word can and need. You must always be honest. If you have deficiencies, you need to be willing and able to talk about those deficiencies. Ideally, you're doing something about them. You can point to a program you are in at that very moment which is helping you bring the deficiency up to strength. Know yourself. Know your strengths and your weaknesses. Feel comfortable in being able to talk about them knowing that when you put the strengths on the scale they will far outweigh any weaknesses you might have.

It's okay to have deficiencies as long as you are doing something to overcome them. A recruiter wants to know that you will take the initiative to improve company processes just as you prove capable of working on the development of your own assets.

The "Why" Questions
"Why?" is the **most frequently** asked question facing a military officer. "Why" is a word attached to numerous key subjects such as: Why did you choose that college? Why that curriculum? Why the military? Why that branch of the military? Why do you want this position?

I remind you that we're looking for Development Candidates. Development Candidates are ultimately going to spend the bulk of their days making decisions. **We ask the "Why" questions to determine how you think and reason and to see your ability to come to a quality conclusion.** As you answer the "Why" questions, the recruiter will listen to how you think through steps and how you come to conclusions.

Every decision breaks down into key issues. A recruiter wants to see the thought process you go through to determine these issues, how you prioritize them, and then how you execute to a successful conclusion. The better your ability to convey to a recruiter your thought process and prove its merit with concrete examples, the greater your ability to successfully transition up.

Remember that both you and the company want you to go as high as you can in management. Top managers are paid primarily for their ability to reach quality conclusions. Allow us inside your mind as you talk about how you came to certain conclusions and the method you use to arrive at decisions. We want a manager who is an independent thinker—who can make decisions based on his or her own thinking (after gathering input from others) rather than on a recommendation from someone else. We also want a manager who keeps the end result in mind and who can devise a solid plan of action to accomplish an objective.

The best approach to any "Why" question is to think in terms of a **comparison**. Compare the positives and negatives of the choice you made with the positives and negatives of your other options—concisely, without rambling.

Tell us, for example, the options you had in financing college—borrowing money from family members or a bank, getting work, or winning a scholarship. You planned on ROTC being a big part of your college career. Let us know you analyzed all those factors before you came to a decision. I often ask military officers why they chose ROTC. The most frequent response I get is that they had no other way to earn their way through college. That is to suggest to the recruiter that if you can't get into ROTC, you can't go to college. Well, I just don't agree with that. There are many ways to finance your education.

I sometimes ask individuals whose major was history why they chose this field. A typical response is, "Well, I thought I wanted to go to law school." My reply is, "But, you're not a lawyer." The person says, "Well, ROTC came along and with that, I had an obligation to the military." I say, "Well, what happened to the objective of being a lawyer?" The reply is that the person changed his or her mind. Now, wait a minute. This person spent four years gearing up to be a lawyer and walked away from the objective with what appears to be a casual thought? No, I don't think so. It's just that the person was unwilling to let me see how his or her mind functions. I have no choice but to walk away from that person as will any corporate recruiter.

Understand the critical nature of your ability to handle the "Why" questions. You want recruiters to believe you have the ability to handle complex, high-end positions. Many recruiters will give you nothing but a "Why" interview. In revealing your thought processes to the recruiter, be succinct. Don't ramble. Remember, the clock is ticking no matter how well the interview is going and no matter how much you and the recruiter are enjoying your conversation.

The "Why" Exercise. An excellent exercise to prepare for the "Why" questions is to write down all the major career events in your life and then put the word "Why" in front of each. Record your answers and your analysis of the issues involved in each of the decisions on a tape recorder. Next, listen to yourself. Do your answers reveal strong reasoning? When they do, you're in good shape for handling the "Why" questions in an interview.

The only way you will become smooth in delivering answers to "Why" questions is through practice. Lots of practice. Throughout this chapter I am going to give you examples of "Why" questions and other questions that you will be asked in a corporate interview. I also will give you advice on how to develop the best answers to them. Pay attention. Mark up this chapter. Take notes.

"Tell Me About Yourself"
The recruiter says to you, "Tell me about yourself." There will rarely be an interview in which this is not asked. I have had people take up the entire 30-minute interview telling me about themselves but not covering the issues in which I had any interest. Some interviewing books encourage you to take 20 to 40 minutes for your answer. I disagree. Many corporate recruiters dislike long-winded answers to this question so much that they have changed the question to: "Take five minutes, and tell me about yourself." I suggest you introduce your childhood or early family situation in the opening sentence (where you were raised or what

was emphasized in your family while you grew up) and then talk for one to two minutes on each chapter in your background—high school, college, and the military. In your answers you should cover only two things—your goals and your accomplishments. **Note: no rhetoric, just goals and accomplishments.** Your answer to this question should be a "bare bones" outline of who you are.

When interviewers ask this question, they are attempting to determine if you are at the "helm" of your vehicle (your personal life) and thus, by nature, capable of stepping to the "helm" of the area, department, or division to which you would be assigned within their company. They want to be assured you're solidly in the front seat behind the steering wheel making sure you're "driving" your life in the direction you want it to go. Too many people appear to ride in the passenger seat, and, sadly, some seem to be riding in the trunk. Only two words can give the proper perspective to a recruiter—**want (goal)** and **result (accomplishment)**. These two words closely state you are in **control of your life** and are working to make your life successful.

I'll give you an example of an individual who had no understanding of the need to direct his life. Awhile ago, I interviewed a young officer. His spouse was also present during the interview. About 20 minutes into the interview, I sensed his spouse becoming uptight. She crossed her arms, leaned back in the chair, and arched her back. I wasn't quite sure what was causing it, even though I hoped I wasn't giving her any cause to be upset. Suddenly, she interrupted the interview in an explosive manner, looked at her husband, and, in a fierce voice, asked him if he had ever made a decision on his own! Then she said, "I can tell you, I wouldn't hire you!"

I admit I was uncomfortable observing this scenario but not as uncomfortable as I would have been had I been riding down in the elevator with them after I proceeded to decline her husband.

Let's take a look at the interview. I was using the "Why" interviewing technique. I asked the officer why he chose his college. He told me that he had never planned to go to college, but two of his best friends talked him into going and so he went where they went. I asked why he selected biology as his major. He really didn't know what he wanted to do, but because he had a good friend whom he respected who chose biology, he thought it would be good for him also. I then asked why he joined a fraternity, and again it was because of a friend. This person's direction in school and in life reflected no goals, no direction. He was not at the "helm" of his life—it was being steered by someone else. His major career decisions were made by circumstance. You can imagine why companies have no interest in hiring people who think this way to lead their company into the next century.

Here is an example of an appropriate reply given by an individual who was asked to tell about himself: "I'm an only child of a Texas farm family. When I went to high school, there were several things I **wanted** to accomplish. First of all, I **wanted** a grade point average (**goal**) that would allow me to get into the college of my choice. I was accepted by Texas A & M (**accomplishment**). I also knew that I **wanted** to play sports (**goal**). I was a wrestler and a football player (**accomplishment**)." Remember that we're taking a hard look to see if you are goal-oriented and have the ability to make it happen! Notice I didn't say goal, accomplishment, and detail. At this point, you will not be going into detail as to why you set the goal or how you accomplished it.

Your explanation of military goals and accomplishments should be brief. **Do not get into every job in the military, if any at all**. Talk in overall terms of your development during your military experience. Focus on the primary reasons why the business world has an interest in hiring the JMO (leadership, track record of accomplishments, ability to get results, subjective and objective assets). Your answer must touch on these important issues.

As you discuss a point of interest, recruiters may interrupt to ask questions. They will want to know why that goal was important to you and how you accomplished it. Be sensitive to the recruiters and allow them to enter in. This approach allows the recruiters to ask you to elaborate on a point of interest that is important to them.

When you are interrupted, it's critical that you remember exactly where you were when interrupted so that when you finish answering the recruiter's question, you can come back smoothly, picking up where you left off. You should never look at the recruiter after elaborating on a point and say, "Now where was I?" After all, it is your story.

"Tell Me About A Significant Accomplishment And How You Accomplished It."
As we discussed in Chapter 5, putting your successes into words is one of your greatest challenges in preparing for interviews. You must be able to communicate your accomplishments effectively. You have not had to do this before. You must practice. Recruiters want to see a track record of accomplishments. Follow the four-step formula outlined in Chapter 5 for how to talk about significant accomplishments. Prepare at least 10 examples of significant achievements you had in the military and at least two from high school and two from college.

"Tell Me About A Significant Problem You Solved."
This is similar to the question, "Tell me about a significant accomplishment." To answer this question, use the formula described in Chapter 5 for how to talk about accomplishments. You want to identify the problem, discuss why it was significant,

and tell how you solved it. Usually, this doesn't mean a people problem. It's a problem that had impact on the overall mission.

To prepare for this question, list every **complex** problem you successfully resolved. For each problem, determine why it was significant, and describe how you resolved it. Become comfortable talking about how you problem-solve. Remember, you want to convince recruiters of your ability to solve complex problems. Corporate America likes problem-solvers.

"Why Are You Leaving The Military?"
Unfortunately, many officers feel they must knock the military. They think they have to be negative in order to explain why they're leaving. DON'T. Your answer to this question must be positive. In over 33 years of facilitating transitions, I have never seen a candidate succeed who was derogatory in interviews about the military or his or her military experience.

It's our position that if you're negative about the military, you're probably also going to be negative about your career in the business world. That's not the kind of person we want to hire. There is absolutely no reason for you not to be upbeat about the military. You have gained a lot from your military experience. You have developed your ability to lead and work with people like few other civilians your age have been able to do. You have succeeded in an environment that is mission-oriented. Equally important, you have proudly served our country. Be positive. I may transition officers to the business world, but I can assure you I am an American first and a recruiter second. I believe in the role of our Armed Forces.

Again, in this answer you should be praising the military for its outstanding development of your assets. How could you knock the military on the one hand and then ask Corporate America to hire you based on your experience in the military? It sure doesn't make sense to me.

Keep in mind we are interested in why **you** have decided to leave the military, not why officers, in general, decide to seek a career outside of the military.

Most of you tell me you leave the military because your values have changed. This is normal as you move through life. For the most part, a change in values is perceived by recruiters as positive. Some of you tell me that now that you have a family you no longer want to be deployed for six months at a time. Some of you say that it has become more important for you to have more control over your career. Some of you feel that you can improve the quality of your life by pursuing a career in Corporate America and entering the civilian world. Some of you desire a career where what you do impacts the bottom line every day versus just in wartime. Every one of these reasons is valid. None of these reasons would be perceived as negative and none are too general or vague. There are a host of other valid, positive, specific reasons as well.

I am not suggesting you use these words. I'm suggesting you follow this lead, this thought process. Throughout this book I am not trying to put specific words in your mouth—I am trying to guide your thinking and your approach to answering interview questions. You are unique—it is your unique desires, your unique assets, your unique experiences that make up the "package" you will communicate and try to sell to recruiters. Recruiters are not interested in a facade.

> **DON'T USE MY WORDS.**
> **USE MY THOUGHTS.**

"What Have You Gained From Your Time In The Military?"
You're frequently going to be asked, "What have you gained from your time in the military?" It amazes me how officers brush off this question—one of the most loaded questions you're going to get. As I often tell candidates, "Let's take a look at this. Cameron-Brooks only recruits military officers, so we could say that a company coming to Cameron-Brooks to hire knows they're going to hire a military officer." It must mean they're coming to us because they want a military officer. Therefore, it must mean they want military officers because of what officers have gained from military experiences. That makes sense to me. Therefore, unload! Give recruiters the material they are looking for!

You can respond, "Where do I begin? I have developed the ability to prioritize, organize, effectively manage my time, accomplish difficult objectives, work with a variety of people, and work in different environments—the desert, the mountains, the cold areas, overseas. I've learned how to achieve tough objectives regardless of what the climatic conditions and circumstances are. I've learned how to take difficult objectives and break them down into component parts and how to motivate members of my team to accomplish those objectives, getting tough jobs done with less." My point is—you have to unload. Recruiters want to know you really have gained something from your time in the military. You might think it is enough to say, "Well, I've gained maturity," or "I've gained the ability to manage assets and people." That's not enough. You must separate yourself from the many other people they will interview. Be careful how you answer this question. This is the one powerful advantage you have over other non-military job candidates. Don't brush it off.

"Why Corporate America?"
At a recent Conference, one of my favorite recruiters ruled out every candidate he interviewed that day. When I sat down with him to review his interviews, I was taken aback and disappointed

in what he had to say. He said to me, "Roger, the reason I come to Cameron-Brooks is that I trust you explicitly. When you tell me something, I just know that's the way it is, but I interviewed nine candidates today who did everything possible to convince me you are untruthful. I asked every candidate why he or she wanted a career in Corporate America, and I received nothing but shallow answers. You have told me your candidates read business books and periodicals. But, how can candidates read *PCS to Corporate America, Built to Last, Reengineering the Corporation* and the other great books on your reading list and not be able to give me any powerful reasons why they desire a career in Corporate America? I have to say I have no interest in people who are not excited about Corporate America." Sadly, I could not argue with him. How could I defend candidates who have studied the business world but could not talk about it in depth and with enthusiasm?

Look at it from this perspective: Imagine you are interviewing people interested in entering the military. You ask them why they want to enter the military. Their responses are shallow, uninformed. No one you interview seems educated nor excited about entering the military. How interested are you going to be about hiring them for a critical opening?

If you are going to leave the military and step up into a business career in Corporate America, you must read, comprehend, and demonstrate intellect to the recruiters. Read books that will help you talk intelligently about careers, business trends and operational procedures in Corporate America. Gain an understanding about and appreciation for the business world so that you can talk intelligently about it. What's more, convince recruiters you are passionate about a career in the business world. Companies want people who are going to be excited about what they do.

Again, refer to Appendix B in the back of this book for a list of books I recommend for your personal development and specifically, business knowledge.

Education Questions

If you have a degree that is generally considered irrelevant to business, such as liberal arts, the question is not whether you should or should not have chosen it. The question is, how do you sell it to Corporate America? You and I both know that some of the top people in Corporate America have liberal arts degrees, but I've never had a company ask me to find them an individual with a degree in liberal arts. It's perfectly all right that you have one. No one would suggest that you couldn't get value out of it. Yet, it does not have obvious relevance to most functional career fields in Corporate America.

Don't get defensive about your liberal arts degree. We're not suggesting you wasted your time in college or that you're not going to get value from it. However, it seems I spend half my time consoling people who have this degree. I want to help you get over the fact that it is an irrelevant degree—it was not designed for Corporate America, for the world of profit. A liberal arts degree isn't as applicable to the business world as finance, computer science, business management, engineering, accounting, etc.— these curriculums are directly linked to Corporate America.

That doesn't mean a liberal arts degree is bad, but it does mean it will take you months to look through *The Wall Street Journal* and find a company looking for a liberal arts degree.

Here's my thinking on how to explain it: "Relative to my decision today to come to Corporate America, my liberal arts degree was a mistake. I don't want to suggest that I didn't get things out of political science that will be of value to me, because I thoroughly enjoyed it and feel I developed skills important in the business world, such as problem-solving and communication skills. However, had I known then what I know today of my desire to have a career in the profit-oriented world, I would have earned a more relevant degree."

Stress your determination to enter the business world. Frequently, in asking a person with an irrelevant degree why they want to go into business, we have to say, "You've never shown any indication of interest in business in the 25 plus years of your life."

I draw the analogy that you have a neighbor who has been next door for 26 years. You've left the house every morning and returned every night—but never looked across the fence and said hello. Then, suddenly, one day you lean across the fence and ask the neighbor to marry you. The neighbor answers, "For 26 years you've ignored me. Now you want to marry me. Why?" The neighbor has every reason to ask—and you need to explain. Give proof and evidence. You can't just say, "Betty no longer has an interest in me; therefore, I'm coming to you."

You will have to help the recruiter understand how you decided you wanted a career in the business world. Give proof and evidence of research you did, books you read, people you interviewed, choices you considered—why you've concluded you want to transition to business.

I remember being in Fort Bragg, North Carolina, interviewing an officer with a government degree. I said, "Government degree. I just don't know what I can do." He said, "I'm coming to Corporate America whether through you or through someone else. I want to use your company because you have placed four of my friends." He then went on to give me solid **proof and evidence** of his interest. "The reason I'm coming to Corporate

America is I have talked with friends in major corporations, and I have read several books (he stated title and author) about business which have encouraged me to make this choice. For the following reasons (he put his hands up in the air and ticked them off), I have decided to go into Corporate America." I listened to him. There was absolutely no question in my mind this young man had done his homework. He was committed and convincing. I brought him to our Conference, and every company fought over him. He now has an outstanding job in the business world, is performing at a remarkable level, and has remained a close friend and ally of mine (as of this third edition, he has completed his MBA and continues to have brilliant success).

I want to comment on one other point that can get officers into trouble. An officer comes to me for an initial interview, having submitted his resignation and stating that he has made a decision to have the balance of his career in the business world. I ask, "How did you come to the conclusion you wanted a career in Corporate America?" I then get a bunch of rhetoric that doesn't have a lot of substance to it. I ask, "How many business books have you read?" He tells me he has read *PCS to Corporate America*, a motivational book, and a book on the stock market. However, he tells me that he plans to get involved in a quality business reading program in the near future. Stop, don't miss this point. What this officer is saying is that the first thing he does when faced with a major decision is make the decision, and then he does his research. And this person wants a company to hire him to help lead them into the next century?

Recruiters don't care whether you have a less relevant degree. They do care whether you are coming to us for the right reasons. You must bring us **proof and evidence** of the research and the contemplation that has gone into your decision.

"What Is Your Location Preference?"

Development Candidates and their families must have a good attitude regarding location. If you are going to climb to the top of a multi-national corporation, you can expect promotions to different cities (maybe countries) during your career. You need to discuss this with your family and determine if this fits your career plans and whether you can embrace this concept with a positive attitude. I'm always disappointed when, after I have put much effort into working with a candidate for several weeks or months, he or she comes to me and tells me location has become an issue and he or she wants to be in only one or two places. This is not professional conduct. Corporate America and I are very up-front on this issue, and you owe it to yourself to be equally up-front. The time to discuss this issue within your family is before you engage the services of a recruiting firm to work for you.

What is your location preference? This question has probably caused more recruiters to get an instant sour attitude about a candidate than any other. The most frequent answer is, "I'm open." But "open" is not a definition of location. Recruiters don't believe it. Don't use it.

There are very few people in this world who don't have a location preference. In answering this key question, state a regional preference—the Northeast, the Midwest, the Southeast, etc. I do not recommend that you give a city or a state; just specify a region. Giving one city or even one state is a red flag in the eyes of most recruiters. Give the broadest area possible—but one that honestly answers the question.

You may then want to follow the regional preference with a statement that you're open by saying, "I am not really looking for a location. I'm looking for a career. If everything is equal, then

I would prefer the position to be in the Northeast, but I have a good attitude about going anywhere in the United States."

Be **smart** as well as **honest** in how you answer. If, for example, you're interviewing for a position in Cincinnati and your true preference is the Northeast, say your location preference would be east of the Mississippi River. That will include Cincinnati and the Northeast.

Never waste your time or a company's time by telling them something that is not true. If you're not willing to relocate, if you're not willing to be open, then say so. Analyze what you're willing to do. Be honest about it—with yourself and with recruiters. However, if you want a development career with a FORTUNE 500 company, you must be willing to relocate. **Do not assume you can take the good and reject the bad.**

Candidates sometimes say they have a great attitude about going anywhere in the United States with the exception of California and New York. I say to them that those are the two highest gross national product areas in the country. It doesn't make sense that you, as a Development Candidate, can eliminate or would want to eliminate the locations that produce the greatest dollar volume for your company. This doesn't mean you're going to have to live there your entire career or even move to those states, but we can't assure you this won't happen. Officers have also told me, "I want to live in the geographical area of my preference, and later I would be willing to move." "I have been on a remote assignment and haven't been near my parents for two or three years." "I want to go there to begin my career." We've heard those statements a million times. Once we have put you in that location, you don't have more reason to leave after two or three years; you have more reason to stay.

We have a great attitude about putting you where you want to be if we get a strong feeling that you are willing to go anyplace. You must be honest not only with yourself but with Corporate America. You must analyze exactly what it is that will allow you to accomplish the objectives you want and proceed to the type of company that allows you to accomplish those objectives.

Again, be sure you speak with everyone who will be a part of your career decision. After your recruiting firm and interviewing companies have spent time and money to assist in your transition or to hire you, it is very unprofessional to tell them your spouse, fiancé(e), or parents do not want you to leave a certain geographical area. Be a responsible person and discuss location with those involved in the decision before, not after, you engage a recruiting firm or a company. To hope that everything will work out "perfectly" is immature and irresponsible decision-making. Our firm and company clients are hostile about this—and rightfully so. The time to think about this is before you interview, not afterwards.

"What Is Your Leadership Style?"
You will be asked in every interview to describe your leadership style. Realize this interview question can come in many forms. For example, all of the following questions are aimed at discovering your leadership style: How do you motivate people to accomplish objectives? Why do people want to work for you? How do you lead?

All company recruiters will ask you about your leadership style in an interview. One reason for this is that there are many differences between the way the military leads and the way it is done in business. Recruiters want to evaluate your leadership style to determine if it is compatible with their company's working environment.

Let's first look at the style of leadership Corporate America endorses—the participative leader. It is critical that you become familiar with the current thought on leadership by reading business books on leadership. This is the only way you will be able to talk intelligently about the way you interact with and lead others.

The perception is that the military style of leadership is designed to be "directive." Some of you are more directive in the way you lead people than others. You can't use Fort Leavenworth as a tool. Unlike the military, business leaders do not use contracts and UCMJ as motivators (these are not tools that we have in business). Don't think for a moment contracts and UCMJ are not influential in the military for getting people to agree to certain things, to produce certain things, etc. If you think that this is not used in the military, at least subconsciously, let me ask you this: How long would a civilian friend or your civilian spouse/significant other stay in a work situation that was unacceptable or negative (for example, if he or she did not get along with his or her boss or the expectations were unrealistic or the work atmosphere was undesirable)? He or she might stay a day, a week? Probably no longer than that. He or she would simply get up and walk out the door. You and I both know this can't happen in the military. There is this thing called a contract that must be fulfilled. It is this fact that makes leadership in the military acutely different from that in the business world.

You must learn a different style, be able to talk about different styles of leadership and prove to recruiters that you are capable of exercising a style other than directive. It is critical that while you are still in the military you start to develop a leadership style that does not rely on telling people what to do. Companies want to see that you are able to lead others in a positive way, creating a pleasant work environment, building consensus, and helping others and their organization become better at what they do. The business world wants leaders who can teach, who help others achieve success and grow. You can't do this by simply "leading by example" or "taking care of my people." You teach others by listening, encouraging, setting goals together and believing in them.

The number one reason Corporate America likes to recruit junior military officers is because of your leadership experience. When preparing your answer to this question, reflect on this. You cannot ignore the magnitude of this question. Under no circumstance can you give us textbook answers. You cannot tell us you lead by example, are a situational manager, or manage by objective. This simply is not adequate. **We want to know what you do to motivate members of your team, your peers, and your superiors.**

In Corporate America the concept of leadership is evolving. In the past, leadership was about motivating people to get the job done, and companies loved the military officer who could produce such results despite obstacles. Though objectives were being met, the problem with this leadership was that it was at the expense of their people, the work environment, morale, etc. What has evolved is a more "people-oriented" leadership style. Today, leadership is about teaching. Companies want people who have a track record of improving an organization by growing leaders (helping others realize their leadership potential) throughout the company. In other words, companies want leaders of leaders—people who can develop the leadership talent in others.

In the military and in business, you cannot implement a new process or make significant changes without being able to get the support of a wide range of people. Because of the military rank structure, if you are simply accomplishing tasks related to your job, you really don't need to use a lot of peer leadership (you just tell people what to do and they listen because you are in charge). However, when you take the initiative to make process changes outside of your immediate sphere of influence, you have to be able to "sell" your vision across an organization (team members, peers, senior officers, etc.). The more creative your process changes are and the more initiative you take to make changes, the more you will need indirect leadership skills to build a consensus and make it happen.

Today, every recruiter looks for Development Candidates who have excellent interpersonal skills, the ability to develop relationships and build consensus. They want leaders who value people and who believe in coaching others to be more successful. I am not saying that you should forgo your goal-orientation, but the business world wants our leaders to have a steel rod backbone wrapped in soft exterior.

Describe your leadership style in your own words—and show how it has been effective for you. In listening to your answer about your leadership style, a recruiter wants to lean back in his or her chair, close his or her eyes, and through your verbal picture of your leadership style, envision you going through your day motivating people in the company.

The administrative part of your answer should be seconds to a minute long. We are much more interested in your motivational and consensus-building skills, which should constitute 80 percent of your answer. The key is to give specifics. For instance, start with the objective you are given. "When I'm given an objective, the first thing I do is take some quiet time to analyze the objective to determine what I'm being asked to do and to identify the time frame for accomplishing it. Then, I invite the managers on my team to discuss key issues with me (participate). I share with them (notice I don't say I tell them) what the objective is and the time frame we have to get it done. Now, I ask them for their input (participate) as to how they see us accomplishing these objectives. I do this as they are frequently closer to the job than I am, and they usually have very definite ideas about how to accomplish this objective as efficiently and effectively as possible."

"I rely more on asking questions in order to solve problems rather than offering solutions to the problems. As a leader I focus on the big picture and the objectives we want to reach and seek input from others as to what we need to do to get there. I keep people aware of our goals and vision. I invite their input. I listen. I help people become better at what they do by encouraging creativity and new ideas and by providing a supportive environment in which people feel comfortable proposing and trying out calculated risks."

> **DON'T USE MY WORDS.**
> **USE MY THOUGHTS.**

In other words, what you are doing is **listening**. As officers tell me about their leadership style, here are the words I hear most frequently: "I **tell** my people what our objective is. I **tell** them the time frame. I **tell** them . . . ."

The goal of participative leadership is to make everyone feel they are part of the decision. The successful participative leader draws out the best performance in others by helping them think of themselves as a critical part of the success of a mission or objective. Everyone wants to feel important. It's the theory of stakeholders. When people feel their input is valued, they are more likely to be committed to the success of the mission. I doubt you will convince anyone that they are an integral part of the decision/mission when you are doing nothing but **telling**. We want people who listen to what others (team members, peers, superiors) have to say.

As you motivate your team members to accomplish these objectives, how do you do it? Are you a positive motivator? If you are, tell me succinctly how you positively motivate. I want to hear such things as, "Often, I call a team member and express my thanks for putting in a 14-hour day, for getting the job done, and for bringing it in ahead of time." When you describe it in this manner, I can envision you doing that. Share with us if and how you motivate. We want motivators who can motivate without contracts backing them up. Contracts allow leaders to motivate by threat. We must see your ability to create a positive work environment that encourages people around you to want to be effective contributors. Again, as recruiters listen to your descriptions of your leadership style, they will try to imagine whether or not it would be enjoyable to work with you. They will evaluate your leadership ability and your interpersonal style.

Think through all the situations when you've worked with difficult individuals who have forced you to find creative ways to motivate them. Write down the circumstances of these situations, what was difficult, and what you did to change and motivate the person. Put down at least five experiences. You'll start to see a pattern in these situations—why you've been successful as a leader. Be careful that you are not describing situations where you used threat to accomplish the motivation. If you tell someone they have to work until the job is done, or that they will have no weekend pass, etc., this is threat leadership and is not what Corporate America is looking for in future leaders.

Most recruiters today are adamant about hiring individuals who have the ability to "permanently change behavioral patterns" in their team members. The specific issue is, do you have the ability to develop your team members to continue enhanced performance after you have left the scene? Too often, we suspect by your comments that as long as you're there to "motivate," your team members will produce. It is important for you to demonstrate that you can change behavioral patterns that will lead to permanent substantive improvement in your team members.

To accomplish permanent behavioral change, there is a process through which you must lead others. Practice this type of leadership before you leave the military so you can discuss results of the practice in your interviews.

First, identify the behavior that must be changed. Many times it is a behavior that a member of your team was not trained to demonstrate or about which the person has not had a previous knowledge or understanding. If I am trying to coach a member of my team to delegate responsibility better, I first must identify the issue with the person so that together we agree that it needs permanent correction. Like any behavioral change, nothing is going to happen if the person making the change does not believe in it. Your role is to help the person see how it will benefit him or her and the team as a whole. In your discussions with this person, remember you're talking about a behavior, not about the person. You want the person to feel positive about making this change. Together you can develop what steps can be taken to start to implement the new behavior. Again, it's a team effort. Let the individual come up with ways to delegate better. Discuss ideas together. Set goals together. Ask questions to help the person see your vision and overall objective. Remember, you need his or her buy-in. Your vision is only successful when it's theirs, too. You are there to help, facilitate, and encourage the change. Lastly, all psychologists say you must practice a change for a minimum period of 21 days before it becomes a permanent behavioral change. Individuals appreciate a supportive, positive environment while they are trying to make a change. Your role should be that of a coach and facilitator, providing the positive atmosphere needed to make the change.

As long as the military has contracts and Fort Leavenworth, they aren't going to be interested in this type of process. Take this back to the office and execute it so you can give recruiters examples of your successes.

Remember a number of key factors. Real leaders must:

- Be motivators;

- Be consensus-builders;

- Be trustworthy;

- Be strategic thinkers;

- Provide vision;

- Be approachable;

- Take care of the members of their team;

- Believe in the members of their team; and

- Permanently change behavior patterns.

In conclusion, you must show where your style has gone beyond the guidelines that the military has given you. Companies want leaders who can "stretch the envelope" to allow a company to produce beyond where it has produced before. They want leaders who can motivate others to perform at their best.

Some suggestions that will help you examine and improve your leadership ability and better verbalize it in an interview are first, to think about leadership. There is a big difference between being a good motivator and teaching others to be better leaders. The more you study and think about leadership, the better you will do with this.

Second, honestly evaluate yourself in the area of growing the leadership capabilities of others. Are you teaching leadership? Are you helping the people around you improve their performance, become better time managers, or become better decision-makers? How many people have you mentored? Write down the names of three people who are better leaders today because of your influence. Are they growing? Is their performance improving? Are they getting promoted? If they are, this is solid proof that you are succeeding as a leader. If they are not, redirect your leadership efforts to this end. **Great leaders develop other leaders.** Remember, if you are not teaching leadership, you are not leading.

Again, the best way to adopt a new leadership style is to learn about leadership practices from business books. I urge you to begin early in your military career to read about and implement new leadership techniques so that you will have results with which to back up your chosen style. You must practice the fundamentals of this style so you can discuss the results with recruiters. Simply to have read books and become familiar with leadership styles is not enough. Recruiters expect you to have used them.

One of the things that has made it such a pleasure to work with military officers is your ability to take ideas and implement them. If it makes sense to you, no one has a better ability to execute than you do.

Explaining The Handling Of Specific People Problems

You will be asked to give examples of specific people problems you have solved as a leader in the military. It is critically important that you give us problems that are performance-oriented. In other words we have no interest in alcohol, family, drugs, or financial issues. While I realize this wipes out about 70 percent of what you deal with in subordinate leadership roles, they are not good examples to give to a recruiter. We want performance-oriented problems. You must use an example of someone you supervise directly, someone working for you who couldn't prioritize, organize, or problem-solve. You worked with this individual who was a good worker and had a great attitude about coming to work but just couldn't quite accomplish his or her objectives. Through your personal leadership and motivation, you turned this average performer into a better performer. Show how you helped facilitate permanent behavior change.

Frequently, when I ask this question I am given an example of a specific people problem someone has solved by terminating the person. The officer either sent the individual to another unit or forced him or her to leave the military. This suggests that his or her leadership style failed. Why would you give us an example of a problem you solved but during which your leadership failed? Had I asked for an example of a people problem that you failed to solve, then I would have expected this example. Remember, we are looking for individuals who have the ability to take a people problem and solve it in a positive, productive way, with the end result that we have a better performer due to behavioral enhancement.

"Do You Micro-Manage?"
Many people miss the rather subtle point made by this question. If you said "no" to this question, I would have to tell you that few of our client companies would hire you. This statement bewilders many people. Let me explain.

First of all the question does not ask if you are a micro-manager. If that were asked, I recommend that you say, "No." The definition of a participative manager is someone with a "steel rod backbone wrapped in a soft exterior." A recruiter can see the soft exterior but has to ask questions to determine your backbone—questions such as, "Do you micro-manage?"

An ideal response to this question would be similar to this: "Yes—on rare occasions when my commander has given me a 'hot potato' and a short response time. You bet I was looking over everyone's shoulder to ensure mission success."

Corporate America is not a perfect world. There will be times your company will need you to handle crisis situations. Recruiters will want to know you have handled them in the military. I remember an incident at one of our Conferences when a recruiter was discussing one of my candidates whom he had interviewed that morning. He said, "I sure like him. He is bright, intelligent, poised—an excellent communicator. As a matter of fact, if I had a daughter, I would hope she would marry someone just like him." I was feeling very proud until he said, "However, Roger, I'm not going to be able to recommend that our company hire him because he has never had his back against the wall—he has never had to manage a crisis situation." No matter how hard I tried to persuade him to reconsider, it was too late. The candidate didn't recognize (or didn't actually listen to) the intent of the question. He heard the word "micro-manage" and immediately tried to distance himself from it.

"To Be A Fair Manager, Must You Use Negative Motivation?"
Your immediate response is probably "no." If I ask whether the military mandates by written policy that you use negative motivation, you again would probably respond with a resounding "no." However, I'll prove to you that both answers should be "yes."

Let's say you work for me. One morning you come to work, and I tell you to clean out your desk and leave. You say, "I beg your pardon." I reply, "I said you are finished; you are fired; you no longer work here. Clean out your desk and go home." Your response is, "Why?" and I answer, "Well, there are two things you are not doing to the standard I expect." Your reply is, "Well, Roger, why didn't you tell me?" The response is exactly on target.

If I had been a fair manager, I would have called you into my office and explained that while you were doing many things right, there were two areas in which your skills were below acceptable standards. I might suggest that I would give you 30 days to bring the first area up to standard and 60 days to bring the second to standard. Also, I would offer to help you in any way I could. In essence, I have counseled you—which is what a fair manager would do. It is also what the military mandates in counseling.

Counseling is negative motivation. While it is delivered in a positive manner, let me assure you people do not come to counseling sessions feeling it is for positive motivation. Unfortunately, when I mention negative motivation, officers too often think of actions that involve shouting and commanding. I do not feel this is any form of motivation. Instead, it is a fear-driven management style. That's okay when you have Fort Leavenworth to back you up. Using "fear tactics" in Corporate America will cause you to have a short career. Be sure you reflect before instantly heading off in the wrong direction when faced with management technique questions.

The Importance Of Being A Team Player. As Corporate America becomes more participative in its leadership style, as we de-emphasize titles, and as we look harder for those who can lead without being "the boss," we look for people who are team players. A company can reach great heights only when its people can work together successfully as a team. Companies want synergy. I've always said that the success of Cameron-Brooks is a direct result of the quality of our team—the sum of the whole. You achieve a quality team when you have quality team players. Simply stated, team players are individuals who have as much concern for the success of their peers, department or company as for their own success.

Some military officers point out that you have performed in teams your entire tour of duty in the military. We agree with you that, in some cases, this has developed your ability to work as a team player. But, not in all cases. We firmly believe that though officers perform on a team, they do not necessarily perform as team players.

Being a team player is easier said than done. Some people find it impossible. While moving up the corporate ladder will always be important to you, a value for individual competitiveness should be subtle at best. The business world expects a philosophy that emphasizes helping others to be successful and to accomplish their professional and personal goals.

I encourage you to examine your team philosophy and look hard at whether you are a team player who works for the good of the team or as an individual who is more concerned about number one. If it's the latter, I recommend you take immediate steps to develop your ability to perform as a team player.

What Are Your Short And Long-Term Career Goals?
The purpose of this question is to determine two things. One, to determine if your goals are realistic and compatible with the position and company for which you are interviewing, and, two, to learn how you plan to accomplish them. This question is difficult and can quickly get you into trouble. How do you know what is realistic in this particular position and for this particular company? What is the recruiter's definition of short and long-term? Ten and two years? Twenty and five years? Therefore, proceed with caution. You want to give answers with depth.

First, define short and long-term in years. Recruiters want to know what kind of time frame you expect you'll need to accomplish these goals. These numbers also will help them understand your ambition and drive. I recommend you judge short-term to be about three years and long-term to be 10 to 15 plus years. In determining your career goals, think big picture and empathize. Think in terms of what a recruiter or company manager would want rather than what you want. It is okay to have "selfish" goals, but keep them out of the interview. What if you believe a long-term goal of yours is to be the CEO of your own company in 15 years? What kind of reaction are you going to get from a recruiter when you state this long-term career goal? It's actually the quickest way to bring your interview to rapid conclusion. The recruiter thinks you obviously have little interest in helping a company grow and succeed. Remember our general store exercise. We're looking for a good "fit" between individual and company. Help the recruiter see this fit by connecting your career goals with results for which the company might strive.

In the big picture, how will you make an impact? What reputation will you have? One of a great problem-solver? Creative thinker? Outstanding motivator? Strong financier? Strong visionary? These are career objectives that benefit your company first and you second. Such objectives are important to any company and demonstrate good maturity and empathy.

Exercise: Defining Your Short And Long-Term Career Goals. This exercise will assist you in identifying and expressing the process you use to establish and attain goals and objectives.

It is important that you be aware of how the business world will analyze and judge your goals. Your goals and objectives should stretch you and make you perspire while reaching them. In the business world, **the more difficult the objective, the more significant the achievement.** Push yourself. Set high objectives, but support them with a plan of action that says they can be accomplished and are realistic goals. Prove to companies you have the ability to meet their expectations by identifying goals and sharing your plans for achieving them and by giving them examples of goals and objectives you have set and met and yet did so by overcoming difficult obstacles.

Beginning with your short-term goals, write down at least five things (both in your personal life and professional life) you want to accomplish within the next three years.

Now, outline how you plan to reach those objectives. Break down each objective/goal into reachable increments. What are the intermediate steps you need to accomplish along the way? Establish a time frame for the realistic accomplishment of each goal, and use a calendar to remind yourself of each step to be taken.

Think about your long-term goals. Write down five things you want to accomplish within the next 10 or 15 years. Remember, stretch yourself. Do a similar, but broader, outline for how you plan to reach each of your long-term goals.

What short-term goals can you use to reach each long-term goal? Some goals may span 12 months—others several years. Think about how each goal fits into and affects the big picture of your life. Knowing your plan of action—how you are going to accomplish an objective—will help you express your career goals in an interview with confidence and believability.

"Why Should I Hire You?"
Let's say a company has a single opening and has interviewed three or four candidates. They all look good. Then comes the question—why should they hire you?

If you could get inside a recruiter's mind, he or she is really asking, "Why should I hire you versus the other candidates I'm considering?" The answer I get from most candidates is always the same: "I'm the person who can get the job done. I have the credentials to do the job." That's what everyone says—and it really doesn't impact or make an impression.

I am impressed with an individual who says, "Roger, I'm sure the kind of people you're interviewing all have good abilities. All of us are confident we can do the job. But, let me share with you something I have that I feel is an integral part of me. You won't find anyone with a better **attitude**." This individual supports his or her statement with evidence, explaining further: "If I need to be here at 6:00 A.M. to get the job done, I'll be here. If I need to work through my lunch hour, I'll be here. If I need to work late, I'll be here." And, "I'll be here with a positive attitude. Anytime you need anything done, give it to me. I'll get it done for you."

I honestly believe the desire to apply one's ability and a positive attitude about doing the job is more important than just having the ability. It is interesting how many recruiters say, "Bring me someone with intellect and a positive attitude and we'll teach them the skills." I completely agree.

You must answer the question, "Why should I hire you?" with words that have unique impact. I've heard it again and again over the years: "I can get the job done. I have the credentials." But, the key is to tell recruiters what makes you unique— your attitude, your creativity, your stick-to-it-iveness, your ability to learn quickly, your leadership ability, your loyalty, etc. Support your claim with concrete examples. Recruiters want a unique response—they want to know why they should hire you.

Be careful not to demean someone else when answering this question. Talk about yourself. Do not compare yourself to others in your examples (remember, we want team players). And, don't go on and on. You'll become boring and lose the recruiter. It's like someone trying to explain why a job wasn't done right. The more the individual talked, the more he knew how guilty he was and so did everyone else. He could have said simply, "I didn't accomplish the objective. I understand what I did wrong. It won't happen again."

Don't explain and continue to explain. It's so much easier to emphasize with a few words versus many. And, remember: When you're asked this and other personal questions, such as why you want a career in Corporate America, be emphatic. Give proof and evidence. Put credibility in your answer.

I like to hear, "Roger, I am going to have a career in Corporate America." I like someone who is positive and emphatic. An answer will have impact when it is based on solid research and clear thinking. You've reached a conclusion (about what you can offer and why you want a career in Corporate America) and can verbalize it. Remember—you must back up your statements with proof and evidence. Bottom line: Be confident, be positive, back up your answer, and be concise.

Other Important Questions
Briefly, I want to cover some other questions that appear frequently in an interview situation. They are interesting and thought-provoking. Take each question, write it down, and formulate your answer following the advice I have suggested. Then, in your study groups or with your spouse/significant other or study partner, practice, evaluate, and critique your answers and delivery.

The questions are divided among the top three reasons Corporate America is interested in the military officer. Keep this in mind as you formulate responses.

Leadership.
"Tell me about a time you convinced a group of peers to buy into

your vision and how you played a significant role in facilitating change."

"How do you build relationships with difficult people?" Think about people in all positions, not just members of your team.

"How do you lead people when you do not have any direct authority over them?"

"How do you build a team?"

Accomplishments.
"Describe a creative idea you produced that had a significant impact at work."

"Tell me about the biggest risk you took."

"Tell me about a complex problem you solved."

Enhanced Objective and Subjective Skill Set.
"How do you manage complex projects?"

"Tell me about a time you used technology to improve a process."

Every one of these questions should take a considerable amount of time for you to determine an answer and the examples you want to use. Once you frame your answers, make sure you demonstrate your competencies and that you make connections between what you can offer and the reasons the business world has an interest in hiring officers. Remember, you also want to connect on the three levels I previously discussed with you—ability, interest, and rapport. Easy? Not by a long shot! To exit the military and step up into a business career successfully takes a significant investment in terms of preparation and self-development, but isn't your professional future worth it?

As I have stated earlier, the delivery of your answers is as important as the content. You must communicate persuasively, convincingly. When you practice delivering your answers to each of the questions presented in this chapter, evaluate yourself using the following questions:

- How expressive is your voice?
- Do you use proper intonation, voice volume, facial expression, and verbal enthusiasm as you talk?
- Do you have the ability to get someone else to respond to your ideas or thoughts because of your enthusiasm—do you excite?
- Can you make your point without being abrasive, combative, or abrupt?
- Do you emphasize key words?
- Do you mumble?
- Are you sensitive to the impact of your voice? If you scream, people tend to scream back. If you whisper, they whisper back. Be aware of this, and begin to notice how your voice influences others.

Chapters 5 and 6 have given you a lot of interview preparation material. Your challenge is to become an expert on yourself—your strengths and weaknesses and the traits that have made you successful so that for each question listed in this book, you can prepare answers with depth and substance. Practice your delivery until it is perfect. Do this for each question. It's a lot of work, but your professional future is worth it.

I encourage you to visit the Cameron-Brooks web site (www.cameron-brooks.com) to read monthly "tips" on how to succeed in interviews and in a business career. These tips also are applicable to your performance in the military. The sooner you begin tapping into this information and applying the concepts at work, the better your performance in your military job, the more marketable you will be when you transition to the business world and the more successful you will be in your interviews and in your future business career.

Another resource available on our web site are the discussion forums where JMOs can interact with Cameron-Brooks alumni and seek advice on how to come to the marketplace better prepared and how to conduct a successful transition. All of these resources are offered to you so that you can prepare to step up into a business career, and they are at your disposal whether or not you partner with Cameron-Brooks for your transition. Use this and all of the information available on our web site to your advantage!

In the next chapter, I turn our focus to some of the common errors we see in the interview, using actual recruiter comments we've received over the years. Use this next chapter as a reminder of what not to do in the interview.

CHAPTER 7

Considering The Reasons For Decline

"Simply having the skills and abilities Corporate America wants is not enough—you must be able to present them. Read PCS, reread PCS and read it a third time. Through powerful, insightful and brutally honest words, Roger helped me articulate my successes and reach my goals. There is no better source to prepare you for a career transition. Listen to Roger. Follow his plan. Internalize his thoughts."

—Shannon Williams
Human Resources Manager
Pepsi Bottling Group

CHAPTER 7 ══════════════

Considering The Reasons For Decline

Over the many years corporate recruiters have interviewed our candidates, I have asked them to provide feedback on each candidate they interviewed and their reasons for acceptance or decline. The following are actual recruiter comments describing candidates who were declined. You will notice that some of the points are similar, but these similarities only emphasize their importance.

As I stated in Chapter 5, you cannot interview successfully without proving your fit on three fronts—ABILITY, INTEREST, and RAPPORT. The reasons for failing to connect on one of these three fronts are noted and fall into one of the following sub-categories: *preparation, communication, energy level,* and *leadership.*

Let's look at the following comments and see where interviewees failed to connect on one of the three fronts and why.

ABILITY/Preparation
- **Well rehearsed but not specific when probed.** The candidate did not sufficiently prove his ability. He talked in generalizations. For example, to the question, "How did you build teamwork?" he answered, "I build teamwork with my team members." This generalization is not acceptable to recruiters. You need to be able to give specifics and have depth to your answers. Give the recruiter enough information so he or she can visualize you building teams and interacting with others. Do your homework.

ABILITY/Preparation
- **No competencies.** The candidate didn't understand or prepare for the competency-based interview. You must be able to verbally illustrate your key, innate competencies without naming them. This is not easy. You must find the time to prepare multiple accomplishments that you can present to the recruiter and that will demonstrate your consistent behavioral traits. In other words, traits that show up again and again in your accomplishments. The recruiter is looking for demonstrated competencies (skills). Make sure you take ownership of your competencies by using the pronoun "I" in your answers.

ABILITY/Preparation
- **Could not relate background**. The candidate couldn't make points of connection from past performance. Be sure to get involved in a quality business reading program to educate yourself about the business world, the different career fields available to you and the specific career field/position requirements. You must have a solid understanding of the business world in order to relate your skills and military experience to this new environment. Recruiters will rely on you to make this connection, as they have little if any knowledge about your military background.

ABILITY/Preparation
- **Couldn't get anything out of her.** This candidate had difficulty discussing her background and qualifications in a pleasant, conversational style. You must be prepared so you can relax in an interview and help the recruiter know the real you. Recruiters want open communicators. To prepare for a discussion of your qualifications, write down your significant achievements that point to relevant skills the position would require, and then practice verbalizing them. Next, practice "interviewing" with good friends. Explain to them that you want the mock interview to be relaxed so that they can help

you achieve this goal by giving you suggestions. The point is not to memorize a canned speech but to be able to convey your ability to do the job in an open, conversational style. You do not want to be caught off guard with nothing to say. A recruiter will not pull information out of you.

ABILITY/Preparation
- **Didn't know what she wanted to do.** The candidate didn't prepare for the interview by analyzing her knowledge, skills, achievements, and objective and subjective assets. She lacked self-insight. Companies want to know you are committed regarding your career direction, and they want to know how you can contribute to their success. She may have thought she could wing it and talk off the top of her head. Be sure you do whatever it takes before the interview to know specifically how your achievements and skills relate to the different business careers you are seeking and that you are confident in your decision to transition to the business world.

ABILITY/Preparation
- **Good supervision, but limited success.** This candidate had leadership responsibility but could not articulate **how** he had carried out his responsibilities and impacted his team. You must log-in hours of articulating your accomplishments so you will be prepared in the interview to discuss how your actions as a leader caused positive change and motivated your team to significant accomplishments.

ABILITY/Preparation
- **Unrealistic regarding promotion.** The candidate stated a requirement for promotion within the first six months, thus projecting himself as expecting too much too soon and not being realistic in his ability to set goals. Nothing will scare away companies faster than for you to make unreasonable demands or to be unrealistic in your goals. He probably didn't

take my advice on how to determine short and long-term goals. It is important to be ambitious but realistic. There are many factors that must be considered for promotion. You will not be promoted overnight. Be realistic in self-evaluation and promotion opportunity relative to your abilities. It is a long hard road to the top. To reach the top, the road must be filled with significant contribution.

ABILITY/Communication

- **Couldn't articulate and give specific examples of accomplishments.** Had the candidate used her tape recorder before the interview and listened to herself, this probably would not have happened. No one can speak in a concise, articulate manner without hard work and preparation. Practice articulating your accomplishments, and support your accomplishments with concrete examples.

ABILITY/Communication

- **Didn't answer precise questions.** The candidate's rambling answer indicated she might not have listened to everything the recruiter stated in his question. Not listening in the interview will cause the recruiter to question your ability to listen to others in the workplace. You must listen actively to every word before answering a question and take the time to formulate a direct answer, exactly as you would in a work situation with other team members, your supervisors, or customers. Good listening skills are key to success in an interview, as well as in any professional career.

ABILITY/Communication

- **Talked nonstop.** Didn't listen and didn't relate background. The candidate didn't look for cues from the recruiter about how the delivery of his answers was being accepted. Be sensitive to the recruiter, and listen to what he or she says. Help the recruiter see how your background relates to the career field requirements. To be a Development Candidate, you must reflect, organize, deliver, and then be quiet. You must demonstrate that you have the ability to listen (a study published by a major periodical showed that business executives spend 73 percent of their time listening).

ABILITY/Communication

- **Rambled. Poor communicator.** The candidate tried to tell the recruiter too much. He ran out of time and appeared unfocused. Rambling takes up valuable interview time and is never productive. You must decrease the chance that you will ramble when answering questions by spending quality time before the interview thinking about some typical questions that may be asked and how you can answer concisely. When you are asked a question during the interview, take a few seconds to organize your thoughts. Answer succinctly, but give answers that have depth. You can give substance concisely.

ABILITY/Energy Level

- **Reserved; low energy level.** This candidate may not have known the importance of selling himself. He needed to show his ability to handle many tasks that require a lot of energy. To make a recruiter believe you can handle a job, you must be excited about the opportunity. You must show enthusiasm and a high energy level. It makes no difference whether you are applying for a position in engineering, logistics, or finance. You are first and foremost a Development Candidate. You must project an image similar to that of the top 10 percent of all managers. As a leader your attitude is contagious. Would you allow your team to be slow? Unenthusiastic? Bored? Not sharp? You must show your enthusiasm and prove your ability to lead others and go the extra mile.

ABILITY/Leadership Qualities

- **No initiative.** In the fast-paced, competitive corporate environment, you must creatively solve problems on your own initiative. This individual seemed content with the status quo. It is easier to go through life as a follower. This is not what we're looking for in a Development Candidate. You must have the initiative to enhance performance without prompting from others. Again, saying you have initiative is not enough. Give us examples of times you demonstrated initiative.

ABILITY/Leadership Qualities
- **Not a team player.** The candidate came across as being too authoritative. Keep in mind what companies look for in their leaders. You want to prove your ability to be a participative leader, one who can be a coach and facilitator, not a leader by directive. Recruiters are looking for candidates who will be able to motivate others by getting their trust versus being their boss. When you prepare for the interview, write down examples of how you have been a team player in any of your school or work experiences. Refer to how you delegated authority and encouraged participation and why others responded to your style. Then, practice telling about these experiences to others.

INTEREST/Preparation
- **Superficial answers.** The candidate gave answers that indicated lack of depth, quality, self-insight, and comprehension, all of which demonstrated lack of interest and preparation. Be aware that recruiters are looking for these characteristics. They are the foundation of a Development Candidate.

INTEREST/Preparation
- **Same questions as everyone else.** The candidate did not listen carefully and did not gather sufficient information to ask specific, relevant quality questions. You cannot ask generic questions. Your questions must be relevant to the

company and the position. They must have a purpose. The better your questions, the better you will show a recruiter that you have a genuine interest in the career opportunity.

INTEREST/Preparation

*   **Shallow questions.** This candidate showed lack of understanding (and thus interest) of the position and career. If you've spent the necessary time to get information about the company and type of career field, you'll be able to do some pre-work. Write out your questions before you interview and practice verbalizing them. During your interview, listen carefully to the recruiter(s) so that you will be able to formulate appropriate, open-ended questions that show depth and interest.

INTEREST/Communication

*   **Difficult to hear; lacked conviction.** Often, recruiters say, "Roger, I like everything the candidate said, but I'm not convinced that she meant what she said." Sometimes, we have candidates tell us they have consistently been soft-spoken. Their parents and teachers have often asked them to speak up, but they feel it is natural for them to speak softly and that there is nothing they can do about it. I have found it helpful for candidates to use a tape recorder to correct this problem. Place the recorder across the room from you, and then project your voice into it without shouting. Do this for an hour every day. You may read from a book or pick a subject and spontaneously give a speech on it. The point is to project your voice. Don't cheat. Don't place the microphone where it is easier for the recorder to pick up the sound. Buy an inexpensive tape recorder rather than the best machine. The key is not to get a recorder that will pick up a weak voice. The test is to project your voice so that soon it will become natural for you to speak in a forceful, convincing manner.

You do not have to be soft-spoken for the rest of your life. I am not suggesting that you transform from someone who is mild-mannered and soft-spoken into someone who is loud and obnoxious. I am talking about presenting yourself in a professional and convincing manner. Watch people you know—for example, friends, co-workers, supervisors, who have voices to which you respond positively—and watch how they project. Listen to the tone and volume of their voices. If you determine after working on this independently for several weeks or months that this isn't doing the job, then don't be afraid to go for outside help. Go to a diction instructor— someone who can help you use your voice in a better manner— or take a speech course. Do not accept failure in increasing the power and the impact of your voice.

INTEREST/*Energy Level*
- **Didn't show interest.** The candidate had poor posture and slumped in the chair. She showed very little enthusiasm, both in her voice and the statements she made. Recruiters are looking for candidates who exhibit interest. Be prepared to convince the recruiter of your interest through your energy level and enthusiasm.

RAPPORT/*Preparation*
- **Programmed answers.** Some candidates give answers that appear canned. You must recognize the importance of sincerity in the delivery of your answers. Do your homework in order to digest the information and deliver it in your own personal style. Recruiters want a feeling for who you are as a person. If you talk with passion, recruiters will be more likely to believe what you are saying and to believe in you and as a result, get a good feeling for who you are as a person.

RAPPORT/*Preparation*
- **Too rehearsed—said what the recruiter wanted to hear.**

The candidate's answers demonstrated a lack of confidence and preparation. Recruiters are sharp. They will see through a facade. Prepare. Don't give someone else's answers or deliver by rote. It will not work. You must prepare in advance to be yourself and to convince the recruiter that you are the right person for the job. Recruiters must determine if you are a good interpersonal fit for the company and can only do this when you are yourself in the interview—using your own words, your own thoughts.

RAPPORT/Preparation

- **Textbook answers.** The candidate might have felt that by giving perfect answers, the recruiter would think he was perfect. If you're not comfortable enough or not prepared enough to be relaxed and be your smart self, the recruiter will see right through you. Would you bring someone into your company whom you felt lacked confidence or, in fact, was a fake?

RAPPORT/Communication

- **Not an open communicator.** The candidate was guarded in his manner and had trouble revealing his true self. How will a recruiter determine your interpersonal fit if your true self is not revealed in the interview? If you have prepared adequately for your interview and have practiced with another person, you will have taken a big step in being able to talk openly with the interviewer. Being open and relaxed are key components to establishing good rapport with a recruiter.

RAPPORT/Communication

- **Was not flexible about location.** The candidate took one second to say he was open but then spent five minutes talking about a preference. This contradiction made the recruiter question the candidate's believability. While being flexible about location may be difficult for you, it is important for you to be certain about your willingness to look at your options and to communicate this clearly. Be sure you have a positive, concise way to describe your position, and stick to it. You appear to be indecisive otherwise.

RAPPORT/Communication

*   **Lectured.** The candidate didn't display a natural, easy-going communication style. You must speak with—not to—the recruiter. Strive to have a conversation with the recruiter and answer questions naturally and succinctly, so you don't appear to be lecturing.

RAPPORT/Communication

*   **Overused first names.** The candidate called the interviewer by her first name too many times during the interview in an effort to establish rapport. Use first names in moderation. Four or five times during a 45-minute interview is appropriate. It's also important to say the interviewer's name in a sincere and natural way.

RAPPORT/Communication

*   **Too much slang.** The candidate didn't realize that using informal language is not acceptable in a corporate interview. Recruiters are turned off by slang or repeated words, such as "O.K.," "do you know what I mean," or "you know." Omit slang or repetitious words from your conversation.

RAPPORT/Communication

*   **Poor eye contact.** By not maintaining eye contact with the recruiter, the candidate did not connect on an interpersonal level with the recruiter and gave the impression of low self-esteem and a lack of self-confidence. Think about your impression when someone with whom you're trying to connect does not look you in the eye. Be sure to practice establishing

and maintaining "comfortable" eye contact with other individuals before you interview.

RAPPORT/*Energy Level*
* **Not natural; too stiff.** The candidate was unable to relax and be natural. You should be able to carry on a two-way conversation in an easy, natural, and enthusiastic manner, which will help you establish good rapport with the recruiter. Being natural and relaxed in an interview shows poise, self-confidence, and maturity.

RAPPORT/*Energy Level*
* **Obnoxious.** The candidate was overly aggressive. While it is important to be enthusiastic, it is also necessary to observe how the recruiter is reacting to your delivery. Be sensitive to any "tell-tale" signs of adverse reaction and adjust. Practice with others before you interview and get feedback about your style.

RAPPORT/*Energy Level*
* **Too intense.** The candidate was too uptight. He was not relaxed. Companies want professional, poised people. No matter what your position in a company, people will respond better if you are relaxed. You must always be comfortable with a pleasant, professional interpersonal style that demonstrates you can work easily with others.

I have given you the most prevalent reasons recruiters have declined candidates over the years. As you look at these reasons, note that you have total control over the majority of them. In most cases effective preparation would be very beneficial. It's a matter of speaking up with enthusiasm; speaking clearly and persuasively; listening actively; addressing the questions directly; supporting your answers; displaying good self-insight, poise, and confidence; and being concise in what you have to say.

Other Mistakes To Avoid

Some other issues that will get you into trouble during an interview follow.

"That's A Good Question." The recruiter does not need to be told that he or she has asked a good question. Unless you say this every time, the recruiter may assume that the other questions are not good ones. Why do people say this? They want to buy time while they're thinking about the answer. It is not necessary for you to say anything. Just take that moment to reflect and then respond.

Evading A Question. Do not evade a question. When a recruiter asks a specific question, answer it. Listen carefully to the question, and be certain you understand it. For example, if the question is, "What is your location preference?" don't reply that you are open. You were asked to give a preference, which is regional, such as the Southeast or the Northwest. I advise candidates to always state their preference in the broadest of terms—for example, "east of the Mississippi River." Do not lose an opportunity just because the location preference you gave was too narrow. Similarly, do not lose an opportunity because you did not answer the recruiter's questions.

Do not evade a question by going off on a tangent of that question. This form of evading shows a recruiter either that you lack focus and good listening skills or that you are purposely evading the answer to a question with which you are uncomfortable.

Answer Up-front. All responses to interview questions should be up-front, direct, and then followed by any necessary explanation. A question that calls for a "yes" or "no" should immediately be answered with either "yes" or "no," and then your support for the answer. Too often, when I ask a particular question, the officer replies with rhetoric, and I must sit there and wonder if this is going to lead to a "yes" or a "no." Have the self-confidence to say "yes" or "no" immediately and then support your answer. When an individual sitting in front of me says, "Yes," and then explains his or her answer, I know exactly where we're headed with this answer. I don't have to wonder. I don't have to wade through the rhetoric waiting for the answer.

"How Did I Do?" This is not an appropriate question to ask. A recruiter's job is not to give you instant feedback on whether your interview was good, bad, or indifferent. Some recruiters can't give you an accurate assessment of your performance in the interview until they have finished interviewing all of their candidates. You should know yourself how you did. You should be confident that you answered the questions with substance and depth; you developed good rapport with the recruiter; you connected your background with the requirements and responsibilities of the position; and you conveyed your sincere interest in having a career with the company. Then, as you leave, you know how you did—you know it was a good interview.

I encourage you to study this chapter carefully during your preparation to remind yourself of what not to do in the interview. Put yourself in the shoes of a recruiter. Ask yourself if you would hire the candidate in each of the situations described above. I doubt you would.

Bottom line: focus your preparation on how to communicate effectively in an interview on all three fronts—your ability to produce results, your interest in the opportunity, and your interpersonal style, all of which will help a recruiter determine if you are the right fit for his or her company.

After The Initial Interview

*"**PCS** was my primary reference guide at every stage of my career transition. It gave me an edge in interviews, but more importantly, the detailed self-assessment helped me choose the right career path from many options. Roger's advice helped me successfully navigate rigorous interviews with some of America's most selective companies. Once I was on the job, the powerful advice in **PCS** helped me get off to a fast start. I continue to use **PCS** in managing my career and guarding against complacency in my daily work life. My return on investment from purchasing my copy of **PCS** has been nothing less than phenomenal."*
> —Dan Allen
> Finance Manager
> Procter & Gamble

CHAPTER 8

After The Initial Interview

Sending Thank-You Notes

Following your initial interview, be sure to write thank-you notes to those companies which have expressed an interest in pursuing you further. The purpose of sending such a note is to restate your strong interest in the company and your desire for a follow-up interview. To help you with this task, here are some guidelines.

1) Using quality, plain paper, you can either hand write or print notes from a computer. If your handwriting is not neat, you should type your letters on a computer with a good printer. Pay close attention to your spelling, sentence structure, grammar, and punctuation. Do not rely entirely on your spell-check software. Check for errors yourself. Mistakes in these areas will ruin the message you are trying to convey.

2) Never ask a question in your letter that forces a recruiter to respond to your letter. You want to motivate the recruiter to take action and make arrangements for the next step, not increase his or her paperwork.

3) Write your letters immediately, and send them no later than the weekend after the interview. Other job candidates will be sending their thank-you notes promptly, and if yours is delayed, the company could assume a lack of interest on your part.

4) Do tell a company when you have chosen them as one of your top companies. Remember how good you feel when you know someone thinks highly of you.

5) Do not start your letter thanking a company for taking the time to interview you. Instead, focus on how much you enjoyed the time spent with the recruiter learning more about the company and the position(s) discussed.

6) Tailor each letter to each individual company. A form letter will do you more harm than good. A personalized letter expresses the sincere interest you have in a particular company. Take a few moments to reflect on the interview and determine why you are excited about that company. Then, create a letter that will communicate your desire for follow-up interviews and inspire the recruiter to pursue you further.

7) If, because of your availability or for other reasons, a company has not started pursuit within 30 days of the initial interview, you should send another note. Again, you should reiterate your interest and confirm your date of availability.

8) I want to caution you. Please realize the massive amount of mail that any corporate recruiter or department manager gets in a day. Why not try to be unique in sending a piece of mail? What's wrong with sending an envelope that is a different color? I just wonder—if I got 20 pieces of mail in the morning and 19 of them are white and one of them is red—wouldn't the red one catch my eye? Have you ever received a telegram and not opened it immediately? Did you ever receive an overnight letter and not open it immediately?

I remember one time that I opened the mail and out rolled what looked like a stick of dynamite. It actually was a paper tube with a fuse sticking out of the top. It was ingenious and unique, and you can bet it was the first letter I opened. In my office there is a small plastic garbage can on one of my library shelves. It came in the mail one day along with an individual's resume. His clever message—to not throw his resume in the garbage—worked! I didn't! And you can bet it was absolutely the first piece of mail I picked up and opened. Please don't be afraid to be professionally unique. Corporate America likes people who are innovative and creative.

9) If you're working with a recruiting firm that conveys a company's interest to you and your interest to the company, you should not send a thank-you letter since your recruiting firm is doing that for you. Always remember that the point is to let the company know you are interested—not to inundate them with irrelevant letters or to duplicate a point already made. If the recruiting firm is not helping you with follow-up or communication with the company, then you must write these letters yourself.

Follow-Up Interviews

I have observed candidates work very hard and be very competitive in their initial interviews. They are invited for follow-up interviews, and they think they're over the hump and on the downhill side. **You are never on the downhill side until you have an offer.** We've seen too many times in football games where a team gets out in front. It appears obvious to them they will win. They let up. The next thing you know, they are defeated. You, undoubtedly, have had this happen to you sometime in your own life. You knew you were in a winning situation. All of a sudden, you found yourself defeated. **When you prepare yourself for a follow-up interview, prepare even harder than you did for your initial interviews.**

I have been excited about candidates I've accepted and looked forward to introducing them to some of my client companies. Three months later I go back to their particular base to work with them on their transition preparation, but this time they just don't impress me. Why? They knew they had been accepted. They assumed once they were accepted they could never be declined—

which is certainly not true. You should never let up. You can never feel you are home safe until the offer to go to work for a company is in your pocket.

Once a recruiter has said "yes" to a candidate in an initial interview, he or she normally follows up with a series of inter-views. You could receive as little as 24 hours notice of an interview trip, and you need to be ready. Get your suits and your "casual" travel clothes cleaned and pressed, shine your shoes, and have your travel essentials easily accessible. Also, organize your corporate information, and keep it handy.

Here are some broad guidelines to follow when a company calls you for a follow-up interview:

- **Take notes.** Write down everything. Take the name, number, and title/job of the person calling if you don't know him/her. Write down any specific information that is given. Ideally, take notes on or in your calendar or datebook.

- **Don't assume.** Candidates have been brought in for jobs or locations that were different from those discussed. Company representatives (particularly if they are human resources/ recruiting assistants) may not have complete information about you, and they may assume, for example, that you know they are in a certain location when you really do not know their location.

- **Ask questions.** Verify what you "think." The person with whom you are speaking may only want answers to two quick questions yet may have all kinds of information that would be helpful to you.

- **Close the call.** At the end of the call, confirm you have correctly recorded all the details and verify all the data you gathered from this conversation. Make reservations; call the company back after checking on something, etc. Also, find out what the company will be doing to set up your logistics. It would be good for you to have a checklist prepared and handy in the event of these expected and unexpected calls. This way you will not miss a point and need to call the recruiter back. Sometimes this can be embarrassing.

- **Be your smart self.** The person calling could be your future boss! Show energy, enthusiasm, and appreciation for his or her continued interest.

After being notified of an upcoming follow-up interview, you must increase your level of knowledge of the industry, company, and position for which you are interviewing. Quality companies have come to consider an absence of such effort to be indicative of either a lack of interest or a lack of follow-through, both of which are dangerous. You should read any books you have not yet finished, find the best library to peruse periodicals for general industry reading and company research, and, of course, get on the Internet to visit the company's web site and locate other relevant company and industry information through the major search engines.

If you know the location for which you are being considered, call the local Chamber of Commerce and have them send you information. Most Chambers have web sites, now, too. Look up specifics on the Internet and in the library. Today, doing research has become much easier. You must take advantage of it. Don't go into a follow-up interview uninformed.

Travel Logistics. Once you have been invited on a follow-up interview, make sure you have your travel logistics completely arranged and that you understand how you will be getting from place to place. If you will be traveling by air, the company may send your tickets in the mail or, depending on any timing constraints, perhaps by an overnight mail service. If electronic tickets (e-tickets) are purchased, the company will send you the flight itinerary only by mail or fax. If you are flying with an airline and are a member of that airline's frequent flyer program, be sure to get proper credit for your flight. If you don't belong, be sure to sign up before the flight! If the tickets will be pre-paid at the airport, you must be at the airport at least one hour prior to departure with two types of picture identification. Some companies will ask you to purchase your own tickets and will reimburse you. In this case you will usually complete an expense report and will be reimbursed before you receive the bill from your credit card company.

Remember that airline tickets are the same as money. You should never discard unused portions of your ticket, and you should keep the copies for receipts. If a company asks you to make your own airline reservations, do not book reservations with penalties that restrict changes. On occasion it will be necessary or preferred to arrange the follow-up interviews of two separate companies on back-to-back days, possibly combining the travel plans. It is very important that you take extreme care to divide costs fairly between the companies involved. You should never see one company on another company's money.

If you will be traveling by car, make sure you have precise directions to prevent you from getting lost and being late. If your interview or interviews are scheduled first thing in the morning, always try to arrive at your destination no later than 6:00 P.M. the night before to ensure getting in early enough to relax and benefit from a full night's sleep.

Now that you have all of your travel arrangements confirmed, you need to verify that every step in the process is covered. "Every step" means your transportation from:

1) **Your home to airport.** You may be driving yourself to the airport in your own car, or perhaps your spouse or a friend will drop you off. Whatever your means of transportation, plan ahead so that you make it to the airport at least an hour and a half prior to your flight departure time. Don't let yourself get into a "traffic jam." If you do, you will be rushing to make your flight, and you will be nervous before you even start your journey. I have seen people miss their flights due to poor planning, which showed nothing to the company but that they lacked good judgment. Plan ahead for traffic congestion, gas purchases, a flat tire, a full parking lot, or any other "problem" that might come up that would delay or prevent you from arriving at your flight on time to board the plane.

2) **Airport to airport.** If you are going to have a layover, determine how much time you have between flights. If your first flight had any delays, will that cause you to miss your next flight, and if so, what will your strategy be then? For example, let's say you know you have a 45-minute layover in the Atlanta airport. When you arrive at your boarding gate at the point of origin, ask the attendant for the gate number at which you will be arriving in Atlanta and the gate number from which you will be departing. By doing this, you will know if a short walk or a fast run is required to reach your next plane. If there will be a distance between gates, ask someone if a shuttle bus is available and if it can speed up your time. Always carry all necessary phone numbers with you in case a situation develops that may cause a delay while you are in transit.

Also, before you leave on your trip, get the phone number of the hotel where you will be staying. You never know what might occur while you are traveling. If your connecting flight is canceled or if you have any other difficulties during travel, you should leave a message at the hotel's front desk explaining your situation to whomever will be meeting you. As a basic rule, hotel rooms are held until 6:00 P.M. for the arriving guest. To guarantee your room for a late arrival, you will need to give a credit card number to the reservation desk. Therefore, when you get details for your hotel, be sure to get the confirmation number and verify that the room will be held for late arrival. If you will be unable to arrive as planned due to a canceled flight, you must call the hotel prior to 6:00 P.M. and get a cancellation number. Otherwise, your credit card will be charged!

3) **Airport to hotel.** When you confirm your travel arrangements, find out who will be picking you up at the airport. Will it be a taxi? A limousine service? Will there be a company representative there for you? If so, what should you wear? And, where will you be met? At the gate? Baggage claim? The curb outside Terminal 2? Will you know what the persons meeting you look like and what they will be wearing, or will they be holding a sign that has your name on it?

You may be picking up a rental car at the airport. If so, you must have a valid credit card issued with your name on it and available credit. You must also have a current driver's license. Be aware that car rental companies have rules that restrict them from renting to individuals unless they meet certain age qualifications. Check with some of the major rental companies to determine current regulations. If you do rent a car, determine how you will get to the hotel from the airport. You must have detailed instructions in hand prior to getting in that car so that you know where you are going. Always carry the phone number of the hotel where you will be staying. The companies will usually make your hotel reservations, but, occasionally, alternative directions will be given to you. Your hotel costs may be billed directly to the company, or the company may ask you to pay and will reimburse you. Again, you will usually complete an expense report.

4) **Hotel to company.** Determine if a company representative will pick you up and, if so, what time. If you must drive to the company, do you have accurate directions? How long will it take to get there? Should you do a test run to make sure there are no detours or other obstacles? Where will you meet the company representative? In the lobby of the hotel? Outside? Who will it be? Have you met him or her before? Keep in mind that even if this individual may not participate in your actual "interview," he or she will still be evaluating you and forming an opinion of you.

Do not leave one step out. Make sure you can address each step so you don't get to the airport in the middle of the night and suddenly realize nobody told you how you were supposed to get to the hotel. If you are given an itinerary over the phone, go over it mentally before you hang up. Also, take at least $100 cash with you, and keep all your receipts so you can get fully reimbursed. Carry on your luggage. You don't want to arrive without your interview suit and toiletries. It has happened before. Don't let it happen to you!

Items to bring to your follow-up interview:
1) **Your resume;**
2) **Company literature;**
3) *PCS to Corporate America***; and**
4) **Three personal and three professional references, including names, titles, addresses, and phone numbers.**

Start final preparation for your follow-up interview no later than one night before the interview is to take place. Then, on your flight you can review the material one more time so that you will understand the information thoroughly. Review all of the information you acquire through research and listed above to maximize your chances for success.

You may think you are an interviewing expert now. You are not because you have only become good at initial interviews, not follow-up interviews. While you should be confident, there are some issues to which you have not been exposed that could occur.

All companies, when hiring a Development Candidate, will want a unanimous decision—having all managers say "thumbs up" to a candidate. It is not good to have even one manager say "no" to you when, in fact, you might one day work for that individual. It doesn't create the best working environment. **This means every person with whom you interview is an important person in getting an offer from that company.** Therefore, make each person feel he or she is important to the decision. You must go to every interview armed with questions for that interviewer. You cannot ask a question and show no interest in the answer. You should never ask a question when you already know the answer. When you get ready to go on a follow-up interview, you need to have many quality, open-ended questions at your disposal.

During the follow-up interview, it is critical that you make points of connection on all three fronts, proving your ability and your desire to do the job as well as developing rapport with the recruiter so that he or she can visualize working with you. Throughout the interview give the recruiter evidence of your ability, your interest, and your interpersonal fit.

Wrap up every interview in a positive manner. Explain to the recruiter that you want an offer. I don't care what the words are. I don't care how you do it. I've had candidates come back and say, "Roger, I couldn't because we ran out of time"—or some other such excuse. The candidates say to me, "Roger, you know the interview went up to the last second, and I didn't have time to close the interview in an upbeat manner." Sadly, I can already guess the outcome of the interview. **You must close the interview. You must let the interviewer know you have a strong interest in the opportunity and that you would be excited if you were extended an offer.**

Please remember, your close must be company-specific. You must give reasons why you are excited about the opportunity. It must also be delivered with believability. Or, again, if it is the company you want to go to work for and you already know that, let the recruiter know it. "This is my top choice—the company I want to work for. I want you to know I'm looking forward to receiving an offer from your company and accepting it."

Once again, I want to remind you of professionalism. If you cannot see yourself working for this company or if the position is not right for you, stop. Don't mislead the company or the recruiters. Thank them for the follow-up interview. Tell them you appreciate the opportunity to get a better look at what the position and the company is all about, but it is not right for you. Don't have them make the offer to you and turn down other candidates who may have a very strong interest in the position.

If you're not sure this is the company you want to work for, be careful what you say to recruiters. You must later be able to live with the comments you make. Be professional. Corporate America is a small world. You want to be proud of your ethics and professionalism should you ever run into employees of the company or the recruiter later. **Never burn a bridge.**

If the follow-up interview happens to put you into an operations environment, such as manufacturing, distribution, transportation, information systems, etc., you must get involved. Many times you feel as if you're simply getting an opportunity to see a particular operating group, but recruiters are going to look for a high degree of interest and curiosity from you. Don't walk through an operational area without asking questions about what you see. One of the most fascinating experiences in the world is to see some of these high performance environments. I'm not an engineer, but I'm always overwhelmed by what great engineers have done in different manufacturing processes. I could go through a manufacturing plant, and it would take me a week to get all of my questions answered. It's hard to see any of these different functional performance areas without getting excited about what you see. Our alumni will tell you that they were excited about all of the positions we showed them. It makes for a tough decision sometimes when you're standing in the middle of a "candy" store. It's that exciting. You must equal this excitement in your demeanor.

If you are interviewing for a sales position, part of the follow-up process will be an invitation to spend a day in the field with the local sales representative. Remember that this person is doing you a favor by taking extra time from a busy schedule to show you the job. Be extremely polite and considerate. Arrive at the agreed-upon destination 15 minutes early. Come dressed in your best interviewing suit, unless other attire is specifically requested. (Special Note: If you are going into a hospital where you may tour surgery areas, ask what attire is appropriate and if you will need tennis shoes.) If you meet for a meal, there is no need to offer to pay, as the sales representative will put it on an expense report. However, it is important to thank your host. You must get involved. This is not a time for you to simply follow along behind and not interact. Remember, you are being evaluated. Do whatever you can to help out and make the sales representative's day easier. Offer to carry a briefcase, park the car, or anything else you think would be helpful. Take notes of each account on which you call. Who was called on and for what purpose? Write down questions you have of the sales technique used or questions asked and the responses. Do not do anything to interfere with the sales calls. Your social skills will be observed and noted. Be polite and friendly but not obtrusive. When you are back in the car driving to the next sales call, then is the time to demonstrate your curiosity and insight by asking good questions. At the end of the day, remember to ask for the sales representative's card. Then, call or write to express thanks again for the valuable time that was spent with you. It is up to you to make that individual comfortable about referring you to the next step.

I have watched candidates spend a day in the field with a sales representative. Never once did they offer to help carry the salesperson's briefcase. They didn't show curiosity and did not even take notes. They forgot the clients they met. You must be involved. You're not out there simply for the sake of observation. You're there for the company to see what your interest is in the position and if it might be a good "fit." Show your intelligence and how you perceive the position, the industry, and the company through the questions you ask.

It's a shame to go through all the work and preparation—buying the right suits, building the right resume, getting through the initial interview, learning how to answer the important questions—and then fail in the follow-up interviews by not staying constantly alert and thoroughly involved. The minute you're on company money, you had better be focused totally on that company. The minute you walk out of your door at home, the company is paying every penny of your expenses. Therefore, it is only appropriate for you to give them every ounce of your consideration and concentration.

Dining Out With Corporate Recruiters
Using good manners and good judgment while you eat is also an important factor in the interviewing environment. I've seen too many candidates lose an offer because of what they did at dinner.

Always finish your meal. Not eating suggests you are too nervous and lack poise and self-confidence.

The company will be paying, so be aware of the cost of what you order. Don't select the most expensive entree on the menu. That suggests that you don't understand expenses. Today, companies can't write off all meal expenses due to tax codes.

When you order, be aware that it is difficult to eat foods with sauces without spotting your clothes. The primary purpose of the meal is to interview rather than eat. Therefore, order foods that are easy to handle—thereby reducing the risk of unsightly stains.

You may think it won't happen to you, but I've seen it happen to the very best candidates. It's embarrassing to have a spot on your tie, shirt or pants, blouse or skirt, for the balance of an interview— especially if the spilling happened at breakfast. Getting yourself into that kind of situation suggests you aren't controlling your environment. You're losing sight of the meal's objective—which is to provide an opportunity to interview.

Etiquette. Also, remember your manners. Since we live in such a fast-paced world, rules of etiquette are often never learned—or, at best, forgotten. However, business is often conducted over meals, and remembering to demonstrate good manners is very important.

Drinking. There is absolutely no excuse for drinking alcohol during an interview—period. If offered a drink, you may say, "I do drink on occasion but not while I'm interviewing." If the recruiter doesn't accept that as professional behavior, you probably wouldn't want to work for that company anyway. I have never had a recruiter disagree with this commonsense recommendation.

Again, there is no reason for drinking alcohol in an interview, and, as far as I'm concerned, the recruiter shouldn't be drinking either.

Refer to Appendix C for interview self-evaluation sheets to use after each follow-up interview.

CHAPTER 9

Moving Toward The Offer

*"**PCS** gave me valuable tips on what to do and what not to do, but more than that, it served as a constant reference during my transition. Whenever I had a doubt or a question, **PCS** was always there with an answer or an explanation—sometimes alleviating and sometimes justifying my anxieties. Now, as I march down the path to success in Corporate America, I often think back to the lessons I learned in **PCS**. The book left an indelible mark, making me a better person, leader, and contributor."*

—Judy Musgrove
Senior Market Analyst
Telecommunications Products Division
Corning, Inc.

CHAPTER 9

Moving Toward The Offer

Big Picture

Let's remember who owns the interview—the recruiter. The recruiter is the only one who can say "yes" or "no," and, therefore, he or she has total control over the interview.

Basically, every recruiter comes to the interview with a pocketful of offers. Your mission is to gain control of the interview by securing one of those offers in your pocket. When and only when you are in the position to say "yes" or "no," does ownership of the interview change hands and you (the interviewee) gain control of the interview.

To accomplish this you must put out 100 percent in every interview. Know you have done everything humanly possible to have a good interview. Sometimes candidates tell me their objective is to convert every interview into an offer. This simply is not going to happen. There are too many variables that go into the hiring process. You and a recruiter might have poor chemistry. I promise you—you won't get an offer when the chemistry is not good. A recruiter might have an interest in you, but during the follow-up process, the position might be filled with an internal candidate. No matter how hard you try, you won't be able to convert that interview into an offer either. Don't set yourself up for defeat. Go into every interview putting your best self forward, and you will be proud of the results. This is the best philosophy to help you move toward the offer.

There are several issues I want to discuss that surround a job offer, from package details such as salary to acceptance or decline.

Dollars And Sense

When you're talking with a company and they ask what money you expect, don't tell them that you're open. You know you're not open. Every time a candidate says that to me, I say, "Fine, we'll pay you $40,000." All of a sudden, they're backpedaling, "Well, that's not reasonable." I reply, "It isn't reasonable that you tell me you're open."

This is an important issue and one that can cause a successful interview to go bad in a hurry. First, it is your responsibility to determine your worth to Corporate America by doing adequate research before getting in front of a recruiter. In the interview is not the place to experiment. When you determine the salary that you expect, arrive at this figure with objectivity, not emotion.

It takes a lot more than simply wanting a high salary to get one. Wouldn't that be a wonderful world in which to live? You wake up in the morning and determine you want a higher salary. You go to your boss with your wishes, and he or she immediately gives you what you want. I'm sorry—that simply is not the real world! The only way you can earn a top salary is by having strong credentials, conducting world-class preparation and having successful interviews. Many of our candidates transition into business with significant salary increases. They are always the candidates who do their homework and execute with precision at the Conference.

On the Cameron-Brooks application, we ask the question of salary expectations. I use this question as an eliminator. Please don't misunderstand me on this point. I want you to get a high salary. The higher your salary, the higher the fee the client company pays Cameron-Brooks. However, I expect a candidate to be realistic about his or her salary expectations. I expect you to do your homework and report a figure that is appropriate and earned. To compete for the best salaries, you must be realistic, and you've got to be committed to working hard in your transition preparation and being at your best in your interviews.

In the business world, you are compensated based on performance. Thus, it makes sense that in the corporate hiring process your salary is determined not only on the basis of your credentials but also on your performance in the interview. Bottom line: prepare to be at your best in your interviews. Hard work will pay off. Research the marketplace. Determine what your value is to Corporate America. Then, set a fair market value—one appropriate to you and for Corporate America.

Pay Raises

There are three ways you can get increased compensation in Corporate America.

- **Annual pay raise:** This raise is just what it says. It is granted annually. There is no specific formula as to how much you can expect in a year (even though some companies have a general formula measured on performance). In all cases you'll be evaluated on both objective and subjective performance factors.

- **Promotional pay raise:** With a position-level promotion, you will receive a pay raise.

- **Merit pay raise:** Merit pay raise is given for performance above the expected norms. This raise is obtainable; however, it is not easy to receive in a world of high-achievers.

Remember, in Corporate America you will be paid and promoted according to your performance. We are proud of our double standard of compensation and promotion. We pay and promote high performers more than others. Our candidates love this concept. Our candidates are frequently the high-end performers in the military, yet they get the same pay as everyone else. "Go-to" people should get paid more!

Being a typical American, you'll never get paid what you feel you're worth. I know individuals in business who are paid $300,000 a year or more, and they still feel they're underpaid. That doesn't mean they don't wear a smile every day. It's just what human nature is all about. There is never an ideal world. You will not see outstanding performers at Procter & Gamble, General Mills, Guidant Corporation and other great companies attempting to move to the military to increase their compensation. Corporate America takes very good care of its people. You earn it first; then it's given to you. You won't get it before you go out and earn it.

Transitional Concerns
We are often asked about career "security" in Corporate America. This is a fair question relative to the perception of security in the military. As more than one officer has stated, "I know I will get a paycheck every month if I stay in the military."

To begin with, during the years I have recruited military officers, only a handful have been laid off for economic reasons. You are being hired as a Development Candidate. Well-managed companies know the importance of developing future leadership. The military, regardless of world conditions, continues to produce ROTC and academy graduates. The same is true in the business world—if we cease to develop leaders, somewhere in the future, we will have a leadership void. No quality company would voluntarily get themselves into that situation. This issue alone should give you good security.

You also should realize the tremendous expense of hiring a Development Candidate. It is now estimated that a hiring mistake will cost more than $64,000 in the first six months! Anytime a company incurs an "expense," it is never taken lightly. As one FORTUNE 100 company stated, "We don't hire two to see if one can make it. We hire one and put every resource we have into making sure the candidate succeeds." This is exactly why companies put potential hires through such a rigorous series of interviews and why they require unanimous consent from all top managers on extending an offer.

While the above facts offer considerable security, we must point out that like the military, Corporate America is competitive. It is essential that you start your new career eager to succeed, to accomplish difficult objectives, and to work hard and smart. In my lifetime I have yet to see someone successful in the military who couldn't become successful in Corporate America. The tools for success are the same regardless of the profession.

Another area of concern is the physical transition itself. Many times, officers have unnecessary anxieties about this. You will find that your company will walk with you through each step. A corporation's normal procedure after a hire is to provide transportation to the new location so that an employee and spouse can search for a house or apartment. While all companies are different, generally speaking, you also will be given guidance on realtors, financial institutions, schools, and neighborhoods. And, of course, all normal expenses will be paid. Always remember that each company has its own policies, and before you create expenditure, you should determine if it is reimbursable. Also, your company will normally cover all expenses that the military doesn't cover. Our candidates have been extremely pleased with relocation benefits. Corporations know that relocations can cause frustration and unwanted anxieties, and they work hard to eliminate as many as possible.

It is always our desire to help you get answers to specific questions. We encourage you to talk with other officers who have already transitioned. Many times, it is comforting to speak with someone who has "been in your shoes." Our online discussion forums allow JMOs and Cameron-Brooks alumni to interact and discuss topics such as this. To benefit from the experiences, insight, and advice of those who have successfully transitioned to the business world access our web site at www.cameron-brooks.com and follow the links to the Career Discussion Area.

Three Thousand Dollars—The Crucial Figure
When a company does a follow-up interview with a candidate, that company will spend $3,000 or more, on a national average, for a follow-up interview. That will be necessary to cover airline tickets, rental cars, taxis, hotels, and food. Beyond that is the major expenditure of management's time to interview.

By making yourself conscious of this $3,000, you can help a recruiter spend it. Recruiters, like candidates, are selfish. Their primary concern, and rightly so, is their own career—not yours. Many times, recruiters are young people who are willing to sit through numerous interviews. While they do, they're very aware that every time they say "yes" to a follow-up interview, they have, in fact, signed a company check for $3,000.

They're aware they can't sign too many of these checks and then have upper management decline candidates they've invited back for follow-up interviews. Before long their "offer to invite" record starts to reflect on their credibility. Too many candidates are unaware of this. You must help the recruiter feel good about spending $3,000 for the follow-up. You can only do this by giving the best possible interview.

If I could get you to write anything on the back of your hand as you go to interviews, it would be this: $3,000. There is

probably no factor that should motivate you more to be competitive during the interview than remembering that figure. I suggest you write it on the top of every page of your notes. Think it over. Put yourself in the recruiter's position. If you had $3,000 in your wallet, would you spend that money pursuing the individual you're interviewing? Would you do it if your career depended on this decision?

Many recruiters, on this dollar amount alone, will eliminate a candidate. Today, many companies are sending two or more recruiters to interview at our Conferences. They feel it is less expensive to get a second and even a third opinion at the Conference. Then, when they fly out a candidate for follow-up interviews, they are more assured the other managers will agree with their opinions. It's a better decision and less costly to get multiple judgments at the Conference before flying that candidate in for a follow-up interview. Also, it assures a higher rate of offer to follow-up ratio. Recruiters also like it because it spreads the risk of saying yes and spending company money.

We're finding companies are increasingly aware of recruiting costs. **So, remember that $3,000 each time you step in front of a recruiter.**

Don't Overspend

Be alert. Know what amounts you're billing to the company paying for your interview expenses. If you go to the hotel bar and order six drinks, you're showing poor judgment. My own judgment, as a company, would be to withhold any job offer.

Think, think, think. Don't be like the young man who traveled to Chicago to interview and then found he didn't have the $30 cash to pay taxi fare from the airport to the client's office. All he had were credit cards. So, he ordered a limousine for $120. You may say, "That was good judgment. He got himself to the company's office." But, let me assure you, it was poor judgement to have the vice president of personnel see him pull up in a limousine, billed to the expense account. This candidate did not get an offer. The poor judgment started when he didn't take a sufficient amount of cash with him for incidental costs. It is logical that you will have to take taxis. Today, to travel on follow-up interviews with less than $100 cash in your pocket would be poor judgment.

A company is always measuring your judgment. From the time you leave your door, you're spending the company's money. You're going to be examined every step of the way. That applies to everything—flights, taxis, hotels, and dinners with company recruiters.

Don't let anyone throw you off by saying, "Don't worry. Tonight is just a casual evening. We're going to chat. We'll be evaluating tomorrow, during the interviews." Don't believe that for a second. Some companies will try to catch you off guard—and there's never any excuse for allowing this to happen. Show good judgment at all times.

What Is Your Definition Of A Job Offer?
You are not assured of a job offer simply because recruiters smile, request a follow-up interview, show interest, say they will get back in touch, or tell you they like your background.

I frequently ask candidates to define an offer. Some tell me an offer is money, benefits, location, or the position, etc. The answers are usually similar, but I disagree with them. These are components of an offer—but still not the clear, succinct definition. An offer only occurs when control moves from the company to the candidate. When the candidate is in the position of saying "yes" or "no" to the company. Nothing else constitutes an offer.

I've seen everything in the world happen between a recruiter's smile and the actual offer. Companies have taken a candidate through eight or nine interviews and still not offered. Companies may say they are going to offer, and between that time and when they could phone you, the position was filled by someone else inside the firm. Or, sometimes the position is removed from the marketplace because of economics or internal company changes and conditions.

You should never think you have an offer until it is, in fact, in your pocket—when you're in control of the interview.

Accepting A Career Position

Accepting a career position is one of the most critical moments. It sets the tone of your new business career. You want to handle your acceptance carefully, thoughtfully, and precisely.

When you accept a position, do so with the primary person—the individual for whom you would be working or the person who extended the offer to you. **Always accept prior to the deadline—never, ever wait until the deadline.** If you wait until the deadline, the company doesn't know if you're accepting because time has run out or because you want the job.

Be extremely upbeat in accepting. For example, you might say, "I don't need any more time to determine I want to have my career with your company. I want you to know I'm extremely excited about getting started. What is my next step?" And, the company will go through the upcoming procedures with you.

I always tell about Janis, who now works for me. Originally, we interviewed her several times. While on a recruiting trip, I called in and learned Janis had accepted. "Is she excited?" I asked an associate. "Well, really, I don't know," I was told. "She said, 'Well, I guess I'll take your job.'" I was concerned about her lack of enthusiasm for the job and even suggested we call Janis back and withdraw our offer. I wanted someone more enthusiastic about joining our team. Fortunately, we didn't. Janis has been with us since 1985 and is an integral part of our organization. I wouldn't know what to do without her, but I'll never forget her acceptance, and I've kidded her about it over the years.

Once you've accepted an offer, you should now write a letter to everyone with whom you made contact at that company. Thank them for their part in the hiring process. It would be a shame if you went to work for a company, saw one of the individuals who had interviewed you, and they didn't know you were with their organization. This is where your professional attitude in developing relationships should begin. It's probably one of the most critical steps in starting your business career.

Declining An Offer

When you decline an offer, don't forget your professionalism. Don't forget common courtesy. The minute you know you are not going to accept a company's offer, immediately get on the phone and let the company know. Don't send letters through the mail. That could take two or three days. Please be conscious of the fact that once an offer goes out on a position, all recruiting for that position stops. While the company may have two or three other people in the process, they can do nothing whatsoever with them. Of course, the longer those people sit out there without being pursued, the less interest they have in that company and the higher the probability they will be hired by another company. **So, never hold an offer when you know you're not going to accept the position.**

When you decline the offer, we encourage you to be honest and candid. First of all, tell them the company you are going to join. What's the big secret? You're developing relationships in Corporate

Amcrica. Let them know. Many times it is best just to say, "This was one of the most difficult decisions I've ever had to make in my life." Be honest. "But, I have made the decision to go to Company A. (Tell them the name of the company.) What I'll be doing with that company is going into such and such a position. I just have to tell you the two locations were very similar, and the money was very similar. I was very excited about what I saw in your company. It's just that I felt a bit more compatibility with the other organization. I don't know if I can tell you what it was. I just felt a little bit more comfortable in the other company's environment."

When you inform a company you are declining an offer, never make location the primary reason. I'd like to go back and remind you that a company put out $3,000 to fly you in for follow-up interviews. You gave them every reason to believe the location you flew out for was totally acceptable to you, so for you to decline later because of location is to say you are dishonest and lack professionalism. The road of life has many curves. You never know when you're going to curve back and run into that person, situation, and company again. How foolish for you to have burned a bridge when you need not have done so. Some-times, it is simply a matter of laziness when you decline a company. What you really meant to say was, "I was sincerely open for your location. I had a preference, which I pointed out in the interview. The other company has offered my location preference. It was the only factor that tipped the offer in their favor. It wasn't that your location wasn't acceptable to me. The other offer was just more acceptable." Explain your situation fully. Don't get lazy in declining an offer. Think about what you're saying. Think about your own professionalism of having accepted their money to fly out for a follow-up interview. Always be sincere and professional in any move you make in the job search.

It would be a good idea to follow up a decline with a professional letter of thanks for all of the costs they might have incurred for your follow-up interviews and the time their managers took with you. Never burn a bridge. You never know when you may want to walk over it again.

Leave The Military Behind

When you begin your career in Corporate America, it is very important that you put your military career behind you. Remember, what's important is not what you did yesterday but what you do today.

Unfortunately, some officers form cliques with other officers within the companies they join. They unknowingly and unwisely create an environment of "them" versus "us." Some officers have done this to the detriment of military officers in general. Companies have told us they hesitate to hire officers because they are becoming too "military." That is foolish. We point out that these people come from different socio-economic backgrounds, regions, cultures, and military branches. Their backgrounds are similar to those of young college graduates who are hired as Development Candidates. However, because the military officers form a clique to the exclusion of others, a perception of difference is formed. You should be proud of your military background; you should stay in contact with other officers but not to the exclusion of others. Do not decorate your office with an excess of college or military memorabilia. Be more concerned about neutralizing your past and emphasizing today. It really is no more appropriate to have your grade school diploma on your office wall than it is your college diploma. These are more appropriate to decorate your den or office at home.

Working With Women

If you are a man, it is important in Corporate America that you have a positive attitude about working with and for women. There are officers who give us the perception that they can't work with women. Sometimes, military officers express opinions in ways that lead us to believe they won't have good working relationships with women as peers, team members, or superiors. Often, candidates will say they spoke with one of my secretaries. When I've questioned them about whether this person said she was a secretary, they say, no, they assumed the woman was a secretary because she answered the phone.

I recall a story of a recruiter who called a candidate and asked him to call a woman in his office to get the details of an offer. When the candidate had received the information, he was to call the recruiter back. He did as instructed and called the recruiter and said, "I called your secretary and got all the details." The recruiter then asked him if the woman had identified herself as his secretary, and the candidate admitted he had just assumed she was a secretary. On the basis of this incident, the recruiter felt he was biased and withdrew the job offer. I'll never defend a candidate who does this. If I feel candidates are being wronged for any reason, I'll go to the wall for them but not when they do things that aren't professional.

Instead of assuming the woman with whom he spoke was a secretary, he could have referred to her position in a generic way. He could have said, "I spoke with your associate," or better yet— "I spoke with Ms. Anderson or Jane Anderson regarding the details." In this way he would not have labeled her with a certain position.

I encourage you to think seriously about the roles of women in business. If working with women is difficult for you or you feel women don't have the ability to compete with you, then don't apply for a position in Corporate America.

Hiring/Managing Diversity

Circumstances have improved over the years regarding diversity in the business world—not as fast as I and others think they should have. However, I can honestly say that, today, most top-managed companies in Corporate America are colorblind. These companies have developed great programs to cultivate and manage diversity within their organizations.

Today, there are many minorities in top leadership positions in Corporate America. I'm proud to say that many of them are Cameron-Brooks alumni. Is it a perfect world? It is not. I do feel, however, most of the people who are prejudiced are in the closet. They better stay in the closet because if they stick their nose out, they're going to get it cut off. Rightfully.

I've always felt it is important to be candid and outspoken when discussing issues with diversity candidates. I think it is extremely important that everyone get hired for the right reason—performance—and for no other reason.

Development Candidates must demonstrate the ability to manage a workforce of great diversity of backgrounds, lifestyles, values, and opinions. The "typical" employee is changing and will continue to change. U.S. corporations are challenged by the extraordinary competitive pressures in the world today. To be competitive domestically and globally will be impossible if the talents of all employees are not developed for maximum productivity. Therefore, managers will be measured by their ability to manage a diverse group.

As you prepare for your interviews, be aware that you will be scrutinized for your attitudes regarding others with backgrounds different from yours. Recognize that recruiters will be looking for people who are non-judgmental, who consider the opinions of others before making decisions, who value people with different backgrounds and values, and who seek to understand and accept them.

Let's Meet The Challenges Of The Future

*"**PCS** is one of the greatest tools to prepare a JMO for a successful transition. Roger is close to the leadership in many of the FORTUNE 500 companies and knows what qualities those companies desire in their future managers. His book addresses the critical questions with which you are now faced. From the interview process to specific job requirements, Roger provides a realistic look as to what is needed to properly prepare for a transition. Improve your chances for a long and prosperous civilian career. Read Roger's book. He will provide you with the tools for future success."*

        — John Matuscak
          General Manager
          Pactiv Corporation

CHAPTER 10

Let's Meet The Challenges Of The Future

Every day, companies bring us more unique, exciting, and challenging positions to fill. As a result, the military officer needs to be even more qualified. In the past, there were often limited kinds of positions offered to you. Today, because of the powerful success of military officers who have transitioned to business and made significant contributions, the development positions for which we recruit are getting more complex. There are still companies that have no interest in hiring military officers, mostly because of a lack of understanding of an officer's background and training. However, I have a loud statement for them: "The loss is theirs."

You have demonstrated success in every industry, in every functional career path, and in every company that has hired you. Let me give you an example of the positions for which our candidates interviewed at a recent Career Conference:

Business Analysis/Consulting

Accounting and Control Supervisor	Internal Consultant
Analyst	Management Consultant
Business Analyst	Operations Analyst
Consultant	Program Management
Finance and Accounting Manager	Project Leader
Financial Analyst	Strategic Analyst
Internal Auditor	

Engineering

Application Engineer
Business Development Engineer
Configuration Engineer
Deployment Engineer
Equipment Engineer
Facilities Engineer
Measurement Systems Engineer

Plant Support Engineer
Process Engineer
Product Development Engineer
Project Engineer
Software Engineer
Strategic Marketing Engineer
Technical Management Development

Human Resources

Corporate Recruiter
Human Resources Generalist

Human Resources Manager

Information Systems

Business Analyst
Corporate IT Auditor
IT Business Consultant
IT Project Manager

IT Team Leader
Program Manager
System Administrator
Systems Analyst

Manufacturing

Business Unit Manager
Facilitator
Manufacturing Management
Production Engineer
Production Manager

Production Superintendent
Team Developer
Team Leader
Work Center Manager

Marketing

Brand Management
Market Analyst

Marketing Associate
Product Manager

Operations

Distribution Manager
Logistics
Operations Manager
Operations Team Leader

Procurement/Buyer
Supplier Manager
Supply Chain Management
Transportation Supervisor

Professional Sales

Account Manager
Business Development
Industrial Sales
Sales Engineer

Sales Leading to Management
Surgical Instrument Sales
Technical Sales

If that is not a compliment for the military officer, I'm not making my point. The opportunities in the business world for talented JMOs are outstanding!

The quality of these openings demonstrates Corporate America's belief in your ability to get results. Each of these positions offers tremendous opportunity for advancement. **You have earned the right to interview for these positions.** You have come to our companies with outstanding objective and subjective skills and executed with powerful results. Our alumni, as I have said, are reaching for the very pinnacle of Corporate America, and many have arrived. Every day I receive outstanding reports on what our alumni are accomplishing within our client companies. It is gratifying and well deserved. It's been exciting to see the growing demand for the military officer.

For those of you who make the decision to enter the business world, I admire your strong desire to make an impact in business and I would be proud to walk beside you and help you achieve your career dreams and goals. For those of you who choose to stay in the military, I respect your decision and wish you continued success in your career.

Tips For Success
In this last chapter I want to offer a few tips for success in any professional career. Push yourselves to reach great heights in your personal and professional lives, whether you enter the business world or continue to proudly serve and protect our country.

Remember, you control your attitude. Nobody else does. All organizations have pros and cons. As a leader, it is up to you to avoid being a critic of the faults in your organization and instead, be a light for others to follow. Don't complain about what is wrong with your organization, but instead do something to make it better. Rise above the circumstances of your work. Act like a leader and people will treat you like one.

Deserve your success. How do you do this? Work harder than everyone around you. Go the extra mile, put in the extra hours, sweat the small stuff, and do whatever it takes by putting your heart and soul into everything you do. When you consistently do this, you will achieve all the success you deserve.

Keep learning. Find any great leader in any organization, and I promise you that you will find a life-long learner. Read broadly, ask a lot of questions, become a master of your craft, and push the outside of the envelope on your knowledge. You should read one professional book a month (no excuses) to stretch your mind. Do not substitute experience for knowledge (most people make this mistake). Anyone can just show up to work long enough and call it experience, but a leader takes the responsibility to learn and grow to gain knowledge.

Don't become complacent. Anyone can have a few successes, but it takes a true winner to constantly strive for success. Everyday, you have an opportunity to enhance your track record. Run fast and hard in every race, not just the ones that you perceive as important. Celebrate your successes but remember that all glory is fleeting. You are only as good as your last accomplishment. Stretch yourself all the time.

Being Professional
To be professional means conducting oneself in a manner that is of the highest standards. We cannot claim to be professional

---

only when it is convenient or timely; to be worthy of the title of professionalism, we must make professionalism a constant in everything we do, in our every thought and action.

Being professional is something over which we have complete control. Thus, we have no one else to blame but ourselves when we act in an unprofessional manner. While we may feel we can fool others and be professional sometimes but not at all times, we only fool ourselves. Everything we do and say portrays our inner self and who we are as a person.

During the course of a normal day, we have many opportunities on an hourly basis to demonstrate professionalism. It begins at home every morning with our significant other, with our family, with our children, with the service station attendant, with the server at the restaurant, with our fellow employees. The list goes on and on. And, it means remembering good manners, being respectful, reliable, gracious, positive, helpful, caring, and non-judgmental.

I am sure each of us can recall an experience that involved unprofessional behavior, either created by ourselves or someone else. It is not fun to be on the receiving end of a negative action, and if you were the instigator of such an incident, you are never very proud of your actions in retrospect. Holding ourselves to the highest standards of conduct in everything we do not only makes us worthy of the designation of professional but also gives us a lot of instant gratification; what is more, it makes each day fun! Interacting with others in a professional manner is genuinely enjoyable for both parties. It is a true win-win.

I encourage you to think seriously about professionalism and what it means and takes to be professional in everything you do. Imagine for just a moment what a great environment we would create if everyone were committed to being professional. Make this a goal for yourself at the beginning of every year.

Integrity

Core operating values. Have you taken the time to determine yours? Have you put them on paper? Do you reflect on them periodically? Too many people say they have standards by which they conduct themselves but then act upon them only when it is convenient. Such standards do not make up one's "core" values; rather, they are what I call values of convenience.

What good are values if they are not used consistently? It is one thing to be committed to having values, but the true test is using them consistently. Anyone can assert they have values; few can assert that their every decision and action is dictated by their core values. Equally disheartening are the excuses people have for shelving their "value" for the moment or when it is not convenient to exercise it.

Not everyone in Corporate America has integrity, but the individuals who climb the ladder of success do. These are people who are confronted with difficult choices everyday, and they know they are measured by the value of their decisions. These are people who do not quibble but, instead, shoulder responsibility. They never make excuses for any failure for which they are responsible. These are people who are unwilling to allow themselves to get into situations where they must say they are sorry. Those who have to use this word often are those who either cannot or will not make the right choice, and they feel the "sorry" erases a poor choice; but, it doesn't. Poor choices are remembered and will have a negative effect on your career and on your personal life. You are your decisions. If you "slide," even on occasion, you can count on others to remember it—and not in a positive light.

Perhaps the problem today is that people are not weighing the consequences of their choices. Too many people, even elected leaders, appear to be able to get away with actions that are unethical. The reality is that such inconsistencies will catch up to you, if not immediately, then later.

In your professional career, you will be judged by your integrity. The first step to integrate your actions with your values is to take time to write down your core operating values and why they are important to you. Then, with every decision you face, get in the habit of checking your options and the consequences against your values. Do they fit?

I encourage you to look at your life in retrospect. I'm sure every one of us can look back and wish we had handled some of our choices differently. After all, we are human. However, we should always strive to make better choices and to become a master of our core values, our decisions, and our actions. We should be proud of our actions; we should feel good every night as we reflect on our day. We should be willing to pound a stake in the ground, draw a line in the sand, as to where we stand on issues that judge our integrity. We should be willing to stand by our values in the most difficult situations, not just when it is convenient to do so.

Recognizing People As Individuals
Learn to use first names. Learn to be a relationship builder. It's important. I remember interviewing in Fort Campbell, Kentucky. I'd been at a hotel near there for three days. With me was a young recruiter who was having a hard time using first names.

The day we left, I told Betty (the server we usually saw in the hotel restaurant) that we were leaving. She burst into tears. Both the other recruiter and I were taken aback.

Then, she explained, "Mr. Cameron, I have to tell you how much enjoyment you've given me this week. I wear my nametag—but nobody ever calls me by my first name. Instead it's, 'Hey, waitress.' 'Hey, you.' 'Ma'am.' 'Miss.' What a pleasure to have someone recognize me as an individual." When she left I saw that my associate was moved, and I've never known him not to use first names since that experience. Today, as president of a company, he still remembers the importance of this issue.

Learn to do this—whether it's your gardener, a housekeeper, or a service station attendant. **Recognize them as individuals.** Don't make them feel they are there simply to serve you. It will make you feel better, and I promise you it will make them feel better, too. When I fly I always ask the flight attendant his or her name. Unfortunately, the reaction I often get is, "What's wrong?" This is sad. Be a nice person. Work to make others feel appreciated. It is a gratifying way to live your life.

Corporate America is a participative work environment. If you don't have the ability to interact positively with people, you frankly don't belong in Corporate America. Our client companies are adamant about hiring people with strong BLT (believability, likability and trust). Does that describe you?

One of our top companies says, "If an individual doesn't have the innate ability to come to work in the morning and say, 'Good morning,' to the maintenance engineer, he or she is not the kind of person we want working for our company." You must respect others and recognize people—all people—as individuals.

One of the nicest letters I've ever received was from a person I had helped secure a position with Mobil Chemical, a division of Mobil (now Exxon-Mobil). I will never forget it. He was very happy that he had chosen a great career field with a great company. He realized that with good performance his corporate career would now be essentially secure. He said one of the things he gained from our Career Conference was understanding the importance of using first names. He went on to state how proud he was that he addressed by first name the people who put gas in his car, who did his laundry, and who served him in restaurants. Today, he never fails to ask others immediately for their names and use their names. I guess I was as pleased at receiving that letter as he was of learning the importance of using first names. Please don't come to us with this excuse: "Roger, it's very difficult for me. I used 'sir' and 'ma'am' all the way through junior high, high school, college, and in the military." I say to you, that's fine. But that was then; this is now.

Knowing How To Perform
People are the most important asset a company has. Companies require me to bring them individuals with outstanding work ethic—people who can execute efficiently and impact the bottom line. These are individuals who get out of bed eager to go to work—with a strong, positive mental attitude and, most of all, the ability to work smart.

It is critically important, as you make a transition to Corporate America, to demonstrate the ability to be a **peak performer**. We want smart workers, not **workaholics**. We want workers who are well-organized, know how to prioritize, and can effectively manage their time to get their work done in the normal work day. I honestly believe that sometimes the military has subconsciously issued you a set of blinders. The longer you stay in the military, the narrower and narrower your tunnel vision becomes. Is that wrong? No, not really, relative to what the military is seeking, but it is wrong relative to what Corporate America is seeking. We want people who are constantly expanding their mind, their world, and their vision and have a lot of interests outside their career.

Don't think for a moment that you're not going to work hard. During the phase when you are catching up (with those who started careers earlier) you must burn the candle at both ends and in the middle. As you reach the point where you are competitive with your age group, have gained industry knowledge, and have brought your education level to where it needs to be, then it's time to bring your work and family life into balance. Stress the quality of life. Don't burn yourself out on the way to the top. Work smart. Perform effectively. Enjoy your new career.

Controlling Your Environment
As I sit in my favorite seat on Delta or American Airlines (1B or 1C), I watch people come on board. I hear them say to themselves, "What seat am I in?" Then, they moan because they are in rows 35 or 39. I often think to myself, "They had an opportunity to tell the airlines where they wanted to sit when they made their reservations. Why didn't they?"

Candidates tell me they had a restless night because their room was next to the soda machine or the stairway or the ice machine. I wonder why they allow the hotel reservations clerk to put them wherever they want. Don't allow this to happen to you. Control your environment.

**WE LIKE
"TAKE CHARGE" PEOPLE.**

Candidates give excuses about why they didn't accomplish an objective. It's always somebody else's fault. "Somebody prevented me from getting it done. Somebody didn't get back with me or get me the information I needed." I scratch my head and say, "Why aren't you controlling your environment?" Sure, there is no ideal system, no perfect world where we can control everything we do.

However, you would be surprised at how many things you can control if you make the effort. It will be difficult to be successful in Corporate America if you don't learn to control your environment.

I remember one of the great leaders in Corporate America. He would never let a problem come to his office except within a designated time of one half-hour in the morning and one half-hour in the afternoon. If the problem didn't come to him during one designated period of time, he would not handle it until the next half-hour session. He refused to allow problems or circumstances control his environment. He was adamant about controlling his own environment. I have absolutely no doubt that's the reason he had the ability to start his career at a large company and go on to become a great leader at one of the top managed companies in the country. I learned valuable lessons from him.

Too often, I see officers who have had their lives so controlled by others that they have forgotten how to control their own destiny. So many of you tell me about the difficulty of organizing and controlling your day. I believe that. I know it's typical of so many of your jobs in the military. It is not that one environment is good and one bad. They're simply different. If you intend to come to Corporate America and be highly successful, you must control your environment.

> **Your performance characteristics are like staves of a barrel. Your value is worth the shortest stave. — Roger Cameron**

Choosing Mentors
Key to success in any professional career is choosing mentors to help guide you in your career. Early in your career, develop

relationships with people who will agree to work with you as formal mentors.

For those of you entering the business world, I recommend you seek relationships with two interior (within your company) and two exterior (outside your company) mentors. The reason for selecting at least two or more mentors is for you to gain from a diversity of opinions and advice. It is good to have a balance of opinions to measure one suggestion against another. While both viewpoints may be accurate, combining a couple or several opinions will give you confidence about the information you are receiving. I would recommend you talk to your parents, family members, and friends to identify people who have been successful in the business world for your exterior mentors. As an alumnus of Cameron-Brooks, you would benefit from having our organization as one of your exterior mentors. From our vantage point, we see what is happening in a wide variety of companies and industries. We share this cross-view of Corporate America with our alumni and make recommendations to them on what to do to continue to succeed in their business careers.

Select interior mentors by the end of your first year in Corporate America, if not before. Choose these individuals very carefully. It is important to select people who have had successful careers within your company and a level of experience that enables them to see the "big picture." If they are not successful, it would be difficult for them to give you the guidance and insight that will help you be successful.

Choose people to be your mentors who can give you quality information in a timely manner. I cannot imagine any successful corporate person who wouldn't be honored to give guidance to a young Development Candidate. Do not wait until important career decisions are thrust upon you before you seek out knowledgeable people to assist your thought process. Be proactive in establishing mentor relationships before you need them.

The quality of mentors you want are extremely busy people. They are successful individuals. They are professionals with major corporations who make significant contributions to their companies—who accomplish difficult business objectives. Often, it is better for you to write them letters regarding questions you may have, or when you do call them, give them an option of two or three possible times they can speak with you. Today many people find e-mail the most convenient method for exchanging ideas. Ask your mentor which method of communication works best for them. More than anything else, when you have received information, take the time to write a thank-you letter within 24 hours.

Early in your relationship with mentors, let them know what your strengths are, what you like to do, and your high school, college and military extracurricular activities. Give them insight as to what it is you want to accomplish in your career. Let them know what things excite you in a career. It is also helpful to be very candid about your financial status. Any advice given to you must be compatible with your personal financial situation. Prepare a resume and give copies to your mentors. Keep your resume information current. The more information you can give them about yourself, the more accurate their insight and advice can be. I encourage you not to miss out on the benefit of having mentors as you pursue a military or business career.

Stop right now and set a deadline for selecting your mentors. Most successful people realize the advantage of mentorship and establish their mentors early in their career. Take action on this point.

Networking
Successful individuals know the benefits of networking. Networking

has become an art in itself. It involves establishing and maintaining relationships with people. It doesn't just happen. You must work at it. You will find that most people enjoy helping others direct their careers and will talk to you and give you information. It's up to you to make the contacts. Look for opportunities with everyone you meet to develop equally beneficial relationships.

For officers planning a career transition, observe other outstanding officers who are establishing careers in Corporate America. Make their acquaintance, develop friendships, and most of all, maintain those friendships. Remember the law of maintaining relationships: "You must give as much or more than you receive." Think about what you have to offer other people that will contribute real value to their business lives, and develop those capabilities. Too many people wait too late in life to appreciate the value of developing good relationships with others.

As you move into a business career, I would suggest you develop your network in many different career fields, such as engineering, finance, IT, sales, accounting, and manufacturing. At any time in your career, you should be able to contact a close friend who is an engineer or in IT to discuss a technical issue or to contact someone in finance to talk about financial analysis or financial planning for the future. I would recommend that you expand your network to include many companies and industries. This will provide you with a greater diversity of knowledge.

Developing A Master Mind Group
Another excellent way to network is to form a "master mind" group. Many executives and entrepreneurs are members of master mind groups. Members meet periodically to brainstorm solutions to issues of importance. The master mind principle makes it possible for an individual, through association with others, to acquire the knowledge of those individuals without having their education level. For example, an IT expert can

explain next generation computer technology perfectly, but you don't need a four-year IT degree to understand it. The master mind concept suggests that there is more opportunity for success in dealing with obstacles to a goal if two or more minds work in perfect harmony toward that goal.

Scarcely a day goes by that we aren't gaining information from diverse, educated, and knowledgeable people, and understanding it   without an equal amount of education. Most of us go through life having informal master mind alliances, usually in an unconscious state of mind. I'm suggesting you formalize your own master mind group.

I regret waiting until I was 55 years old to form a master mind group. I have received many direct benefits, allowing me to save many hours of frustration and to accomplish personal and professional goals more quickly and more efficiently. I hope I have contributed to others in my master mind groups, as well. Don't put the master mind idea on a back burner. Take advantage of the synergy gained from such an alliance.

One of the major goals of a corporate master mind group is to help the members do as much as possible to improve their opportunities to have successful careers. For example, your group may want to address specific career opportunities in your field and discuss how members of the group can achieve higher performance.

Be selective about who will be a member of your group. Choose people with similar interests, who have the intelligence and enthusiasm to contribute significantly to the group and who have been successful in the past. Select people from all geographical areas and career paths. Friends may or may not be appropriate choices. Consider inviting alumni from your college who have worked in the business world to be members, keeping in mind that those individuals must see value in being part of the group.

> **Early in your career, it is what you know;**
> **Then, it becomes whom you know;**
> **Finally, it changes to who knows you.**

Your group may want to invite people to speak on topics of importance to you and, afterwards, to answer questions from the group. Consider pooling resources and hiring training consultants who deliver business seminars to instruct your group. The opportunities are endless. The point is that as a group you have exciting ideas to explore.

If, for some reason, any individuals do not fit in the group, be firm about asking them to drop their membership. The key is to have an extremely compatible, supportive group, with members who are enthusiastic about meeting the objectives of the group.

As a member of a master mind group, maintain a positive attitude at all times. Your goal is to facilitate a supportive, cooperative, and helpful group dynamic in order to encourage information sharing.

Your group can be as large or as small as you like. The larger the group, the longer you need to meet so that everyone can have time to contribute. Establish a specific time each week, every two weeks, or monthly for the meeting. Development Candidates have busy schedules during the day. Trying to set up meetings during this time will be difficult. Try early morning (6:30 A.M.) or late in the evening (7:30 P.M.) when most of the members might be able to attend.

Let's Get Motivated

I truly believe God has given us the right to get out of bed in the morning and be happy or unhappy. It's our choice, but there are a lot of people who must not realize they have this choice. Being in the business of recruiting and evaluating people, I observe people wherever I go—airports, hotels, athletic activities, and meetings. I have been saddened many times by people who feel the burden of the world is planted squarely on their shoulders. Whenever I have had that feeling, I have forced myself to lift my head and look at others less fortunate. I have never had to look very far—usually only within a few feet. I would then ask myself, "Do I have the right to feel sorry for myself?" Interestingly enough, 99 times out of 100, the answer was "no." I love getting out of bed in the morning. I love what I do. I love meeting people. I love the challenges that come to me every day. I like the fact that I can meet challenges head on, look them straight in the eye, and rarely fail. It's fun to be successful. It's fun to be alive. It's fun to know I can make things happen. If I visualize what I want, I can get it. I am like the majority of the world's population. I have average skills. But, I have performed far above average because of one factor—desire.

I interview many outstanding men and women who have had but a fraction of the success they could have had with all of their great credentials, and I think, "How sad." People come to me and tell me they should be successful because of their great abilities. I'm very quick to point out they can go to any unemployment line in America and find people with equally as much ability, maybe even more. But, because of the lack of desire to apply those abilities, they are in the unemployment line. I believe that 99.9 percent of them are there because they lack the desire to apply God-given abilities. I have an acquaintance who has been very successful and is quite wealthy, yet he was born with a severe handicap. We read stories, many stories, about this type of person—the individual who won't accept a physical handicap as an excuse not to be successful. Many of us complain that we don't have everything we want. We can look around and see those people who have a lot less than we have from the standpoint of intellect, appearance, or physical features, yet they are more successful than we are. Ever wonder why? Do you have any doubt it is simply a greater **desire** to succeed?

Many people never take responsibility for their own actions. They are the people who continually have less than great officer evaluations, and yet not one of these evaluations is their fault. They're the people who will get to the end of life, look back, and feel that life cheated them because they didn't receive everything that was due them. I disagree with all of those thoughts. There is absolutely nothing you can't do if you envision your ability to do it. As I have said in this book before, you must have a make-it-happen personality. I often remember the quote, "Five percent of the people make it happen, 10 percent of the people watch things happen, and the other 85 percent don't care what happens." I believe this to be true. I stated earlier that, as I interview military officers around the world, I accept approximately 12 percent. I don't wonder why—I know why!

I often want to take young officers and say, "Are you aware you are cheating yourself? Are you aware you are letting seconds, minutes, days, weeks, and months of your life go by and not living life to the fullest? You're not reaching out to learn, grow, do, and have. Why are you doing that? Why did you get up this morning choosing to be unhappy versus happy? What was your reasoning?"

I remember being at a Conference in Austin, Texas. A new corporate recruiter came to me in the middle of the day, and the question she asked was, "Roger, who pays for the candidates to come to the Conference?" I said, "The candidates pay their own way." She asked, "Who pays for their room and board?" I said, "The candidates pay for their room and board." She replied,

"Well, why would a young man fly all the way from Colorado Springs to Austin to interview and show absolutely no enthusiasm or excitement? I had to turn off my air conditioner in order to hear him. He interviewed as if someone should give him an offer just because he showed up! As a matter of fact, I suggested to him that if he thought Corporate America was simply going to hire him because of his credentials, then why was he here? Why didn't he just send a resume? After all, we could see his credentials on a resume. We would just send him an offer or a decline through the mail." This is a true story, and one that is embarrassing to me. After all, I had recruited him to begin with—obviously, I shared in the failure.

It is hard for me to imagine why anybody would spend $5, let alone $450 or more, to travel across the country and not accomplish the ultimate objective. This young man interviewed with 11 companies, and 11 companies declined him basically for the same reason. He didn't demonstrate the leadership qualities to be a Development Candidate. He just didn't act as if he was excited to be alive. I guess he didn't believe he had a choice when he got out of bed in the morning.

As I look at a candidate's interests and hobbies, I smile when I find an individual who is reading motivational books. When this officer comes in front of me, I'm just a little bit biased. Even before I start interviewing, the candidate is a step up in the interviewing process. In 60 plus years of life, I couldn't begin to count all of the motivational books I have read. I can honestly tell you I have never read one that didn't teach me something new. I also have never read one that didn't remind me of things I had failed to do in my life on a day-to-day basis.

Candidates often say, "Oh, I know all that stuff." Knowing it is irrelevant. The question is, "Do you use it? Do you really believe you can be what you want to be? Do you really believe you have the power within yourself to become a tremendous success? Do you really believe you can be a great success—not only in the military but also in Corporate America? Do you really believe you can achieve those private goals?" I'm here to tell you that you can—if you really believe.

Individuals have said to me, "Well, I don't believe in motivational books. I am what I am." That's an interesting statement, isn't it? I am what I am. What these individuals have just said to me and the rest of the world is that they can't improve. Whatever God created them to be, then that's the end of it. This is not true. We can improve ourselves. We can grow. Let me say again—we are adamant about finding people who are growable, people who are eager to become better. They know their success is totally within their own hands. Whatever they want to make of themselves, they can.

I would like to see more officers take advantage of information and motivational seminars. I know you take advantage of them when they are sponsored through the military, but I encourage you to attend some additional ones on your own. I am pleased at the number of our candidates who get involved with Toastmasters International. This is a very good program to help you with public speaking as well as your verbal communication skills.

My favorite seminar is "The Power of Persuasion" taught by Walter Hailey, Jr., of Planned Marketing Associates in Hunt, Texas. Walter is a personal friend of mine and an inspiration to me. Today, in his 60's he has more enthusiasm than the majority of the candidates I interview.

Walter teaches "The Power of Persuasion" to people all over the world. His "boot camp" is an exciting course. You cannot complete this course without knowing more about yourself. You cannot complete this course without being excited about developing your God-given talents. Anyone interested in attending his weekend course may contact our company. We'd be happy to put you in touch with him, or you'll find him written up in many periodicals and newspapers across America.

There are more than one or two self-development seminars available. There are many. Zig Ziglar does a great job of developing the latent talents of individuals. So does Tom Peters, Anthony Robbins, and Dale Carnegie. You don't have to attend a course. You can read books, rent training videos, or purchase motivational cassette tapes. Each of the speakers I mentioned above has a web site worth exploring. However, I recommend attending the seminars in person. Interacting with others, seeing how others accomplish their goals, and meeting people from other career fields can be an additional source of knowledge and inspiration. Many of these companies, like Franklin Covey Co. and dreamlife, inc., offer online discussion forums on their web sites where you can interact with others and discuss topics such as those put forth in Covey's popular book, *The Seven Habits of Highly Effective People.*

I love life. I enjoy working with positive, motivated people. You will rarely see an officer I accept who isn't excited, motivated, eager to improve, and professionally self-confident. That's exactly the quality person Corporate America is paying me to recruit.

As I reflect on the individuals I have recruited for Corporate America, all of them, with few exceptions, have been outstanding. The most dynamic and successful officers take time to grow, learn, and broaden their knowledge base. They don't allow "busy" factors in life to prevent them from doing so.

God only gives us one chance on this earth. If I could motivate just one person who reads this book to reach down inside to find ways to improve, the book will have been a success. I have absolutely no doubt that the book will make people better interviewees, but I would hope for much more than that. I would like to think the book would improve your can-do attitude. I would like to think the book would allow you to choose the better of the two options you have every morning and live it. Remember, when life is over and you look back, no one will have cheated you if you have not accomplished what you had hoped to accomplish. You will have cheated yourself. Don't let that happen. Every day that goes by is a day you will never be able to live over again.

Tomorrow morning, when you wake up and have the choice to make it a good day or a bad day, make the right decision. I know an individual who every morning when she leaves her bedroom, crosses an imaginary line on the floor outside her bedroom door. As she crosses that line, she is consciously aware it is her choice to make her day whatever she wants it to be. I have rarely seen her not accomplish her objective. Every day is a positive day. She is motivated. She accomplishes difficult objectives. At the end of the day, she feels good about reaching the goals she has established for herself. Put that line outside of your bedroom door. Be conscious of your choices as you step across that line every day.

In conclusion, I strongly recommend you take firm control. Be a catalyst, and motivate yourself to accomplish the objectives you want for yourself and your family. Read motivational books. Listen to motivational tapes. Get inspired. Consider spending some money early in your career on seminars to learn from some of the very best America has to offer. Most of all, when you wake up in the morning, be sure you make the right decision.

Marching Orders
During the course of this book, I have suggested ways to handle certain questions and situations. **Under no circumstances am I suggesting that you use my words.** Every thought and every

idea should be digested and put into your own words, with your own manner of delivery. No recruiter wants a person to use someone else's words. There may be certain cases where words are used from a phrase, but we encourage candidates to be themselves. You are a unique individual, and you must interview as that unique individual.

I want you to remember that you're an outstanding individual in your own right. This book has been designed to improve your interviewing ability—not to necessarily change you as an individual. I encourage you to give serious thought as to what you want to do with your life. If that means coming to Corporate America or having a career in a different field, this book will help you (regardless of the field).

Remember, you have several selves—you at your best, you at your average, and you at your worst. Interview at your best. To be your best at anything you do, you must be thoroughly prepared. Be committed to what you're doing; focus and concentrate on your objective.

I encourage you to start early to prepare for any difficult objective. Don't wait until the last minute. Prepare as early as you can in your career for any potential changes you might make. Be conscious, as you go through your military career, of what you do specifically, individually, and uniquely to motivate members of your team. While the military gives you leadership guidance, they don't restrict you from personalizing methods of motivation. Be conscious of the individual people problems you have solved along the way. Be performance-oriented. Be conscious of non-people problems you've solved and know how you've solved them. Be aware of the skills you use—organizational ability, prioritizing, consensus building, time management, etc.—and the procedure you go through each time you solve any problem. Become conscious of your methodology in everything you do.

Use a tape recorder to verbalize answers before you get in front of the colonel, the general, or anyone else. Never be embarrassed by the fact that you must practice to be concise and articulate. Preparation for anything you do in life only makes you a better person. I've never heard of anyone who gained success in becoming a better officer, a better marksman, a better skier, or a better speaker without practice. I've never known preparation to be embarrassing. All I have ever heard in my 60-plus years of living is, "Boy, that person really worked hard to be successful." That's right. That's exactly what it takes.

Pursue your career with a high degree of enthusiasm. Have self-confidence and poise in knowing yourself. I encourage you to become consciously aware of who you are. Have accurate self-insight. Be able to communicate in a forceful manner so we will not only hear what you say but we will believe it as well.

Know what you have done in the military and what has made you successful. The better you know yourself, the better you know how you have accomplished difficult objectives and the better you can apply that formula to any career objective—in Corporate America, civil service, or your own business.

I hope you've enjoyed this book. I hope you feel better prepared now that you have read it. However, no one book makes a well-prepared candidate for stepping up into a business career. I encourage you to read as many books on Corporate America as you can get your hands on. You can go to any bookstore (online or on the street corner) and find a host of books to read. If you have true enthusiasm for a career in Corporate America, it is very easy to learn about it. You can go into any Holiday Inn, Sheraton, or Marriott and meet business people at the lunch table. Introduce yourself. Tell them who you are. I've never known anyone in Corporate America who wouldn't take the time to explain what the business world is all about. They'll be happy to talk to you and give you some insight. People love talking about what they do. Take advantage of every opportunity. Make things happen. Best of luck to you!

To All Military Officers:

Whether you have made the decision to transition to the business world or are simply considering your career options, Cameron-Brooks is available to discuss and evaluate your marketability. We will tell you the dollar value of your credentials and the probable business career fields for which you are qualified. You can be assured of a candid evaluation and extremely knowledgeable, constructive advice.

I strongly encourage you to contact us early in your military career. We will then have the opportunity to suggest certain skill enhancements, additional formal education, specific military assignments, and the best time for you to transition to the business world with your particular skills. Should you decide to remain in the military, the advice we offer will enhance your military career.

Our Development and Preparation Program is regarded as the very best career transition training available. The earlier you get involved in our program and the more time you spend with us, the more marketable you become and the smoother your transition will be. We continually receive outstanding comments about our preparation program—not only in terms of interviewing skill development but also for the long-term positive effect it has on your career. Any officer can transition out of the military. Our program helps candidates step up into a business career. **We give you the tools for a successful transition and for long-term success in your new business career.**

Our reputation is established on both sides of our business—among military officers and FORTUNE 500 companies. We have a track record for successfully working with thousands of officers from all branches of the military and with backgrounds from engineering to liberal arts. We know our business. We know what it takes to conduct a successful career search and transition. We know what kind of talent our client companies are looking for in Development Candidates and consistently bring them the best of the best.

The best measurement of our success is your success. Cameron-Brooks is acknowledged for the professional, caring involvement our entire team devotes to each of our candidates. We sincerely care about you and your career and welcome the opportunity to partner with you and help you achieve your career goals.

Today, it is virtually impossible to transition to the business world without being touched by the Cameron-Brooks Alumni Association. Cameron-Brooks alumni offer advice and insight as you prepare for a transition; they attend our Career Conferences to interview and hire you; and they are there to welcome you on the first day of your business career. The Cameron-Brooks Alumni Association boasts successful business people in positions from every possible functional area and with companies from every possible sector of industry. Our alumni have made a powerful impact on Corporate America. They have quickly moved up into key positions within their companies, and they have paved a limitless road for success for talented military officers to follow. Our alumni are as loyal to us as we are to them. Together we are accomplishing great things in the business world, bringing new talent to companies and helping great companies become even greater.

Trust Cameron-Brooks to help you maximize your marketability and position you for a successful professional future. For more information about our career search services, please visit our web site at **www.cameron-brooks.com** or call our office toll-free in the U.S. at 1-800-222-9235 or from Germany, 0800-85-22670. We are eager to help you in any way we can. Together, we can "make it happen!"

Roger Cameron
and the Cameron-Brooks Team

Appendix A

LIST OF KEY COMPETENCIES

The following is a compilation of key characteristics and/or competencies (competencies being consistently demonstrated characteristics) our client companies look for in Development Candidates. Use this list to help you determine your assets and specifically, those that are valued by recruiters. You do not need to possess all of these characteristics or competencies. My intent in providing this list is to help you think about and determine the characteristics and competencies you possess, as well as the ones you want to further establish while preparing for a transition to business, and to know which ones are most important to bring to light in an interview.

Ability to develop others	Motivating others
Ability to learn quickly	Negotiating
Action-oriented	Openness
Approachable	Organizational agility/ability
Assertive	Patience
Astute	Peer Relationships
Business acumen	Perseverance
Career ambition	Planning ability
Caring	Poise
Compassion	Political savvy
Composure	Positive attitude
Conflict management	Presentation skills
Consensus-building skills	Priority setting
Creative	Problem-solving
Customer focus	Process management
Dealing with ambiguity	Project management
Decision-making skills	Self-confidence
Delegation	Self-development
Drive for results	Self-knowledge
Empathetic	Self-starter
Energetic	Sensitivity
Ethical	Sizing up people
Fair	Standing alone
Goal-oriented	Strategic agility/Strategic thinking skills
Hard-working	Team-building skills
Humor	Technical aptitude/learning/skills
Innovative	Time management
Integrity	Tough-mindedness
Intellectual horsepower	Trustworthy
Interpersonal savvy	Understanding others
Leadership	Values
Listening	Visionary
Managing and measuring	Willingness to learn new things
Managing diversity	Work/life balance
Managing through systems	Written communication skills
Maturity/Emotional IQ	

Appendix B

RECOMMENDED READING LIST

Reading business books is one of the most important steps in preparing for a transition to the business world. It will increase your knowledge of and interest in the business world and provide the foundation for all of your transition and interview preparation. Even if you are simply examining your options in the business world, start today to educate yourself about the business world. Knowledge is key to making the career decision that is right for you.

Corporate America wants broad-minded, well-read people. As a Development Candidate, you must be committed to enhancing your knowledge base and skill package every year. Having the knowledge to step into another area of expertise will open doors for you. There have been more buy-outs, mergers and changes to companies than ever before in history and the only way to guarantee yourself a leadership role with today's ever-changing and growing company is if you bring to the table a broad skill package. One of the best ways to continually enhance your knowledge base and skill package is through a habit of daily professional reading.

Cameron-Brooks alumni will agree with me that reading about business trends and practices is, actually, pleasurable because we love reading about better ways to run our businesses, motivate our teams and improve our services and we love reading about other cutting edge thinkers and successful business leaders. If you have made the decision to transition to Corporate America, I would hope you find reading about business leaders and issues motivating and pleasurable. If you don't, you need to reevaluate which career direction is right for you.

Stop saying you do not have time to read! Every senior military officer and corporate leader will tell you that you do not have time NOT to read.

To cultivate a habit of daily business reading, I recommend you establish reading goals for yourself that are specific. Set aside time every day to read—20 minutes a day, an hour a day, three hours a day (one hour in the morning, a half-hour at noon and one and a half-hour in the evening). At a minimum, I recommend you set a goal to read one quality business book each month. Under no circumstances do I believe this to be adequate, but it is a start and will get you headed in the right direction. As your reading habits develop, increase the number of books you read.

Subscribe to *FORTUNE* magazine and study every issue cover to cover. I recommend *FORTUNE* over other magazines because it offers articles describing broad business trends that will help you make a good decision regarding the business world as well as impact in your interviews.

Also, begin a habit of daily perusal of *USA Today* or *The Wall Street Journal*, plus a regional newspaper. The idea is to obtain regional as well as broad national news.

If you are a slow reader, get help. Take an evening speed reading class. I guarantee developing a habit of daily professional reading will prove extremely beneficial to you.

I also highly recommend you invest in yourself by taking advantage of the many personal and professional growth seminars offered around the country by companies and business leaders like Franklin Covey Co., The Tom Peters Group, Zig Ziglar Corporation, Planned Marketing Associates and Anthony Robbins (founder of dreamlife, inc.). (Many seminars also are available for purchase on cassette tape.)

The books listed below are current in business, and I recommend them to you. However, they are under no circumstances the only ones you should read. Expand your reading program by researching books online through sites like amazon.com or reading reviews of business books and authors in national and regional newspapers.

Following each title are comments which explain why I feel the book is important.

Beyond Reengineering (**Hammer**). Hammer's sequel to *Reengineering the Corporation*. Covers the next generation of reengineering and its effects on Corporate America.

Built to Last (**Collins and Porras**). A valuable book regardless of your career path. Discusses with clarity the distinguishing characteristics of the world's most enduring and successful corporations.

The Deming Management Method (**Walton**). An easy-to-read book on Deming's Total Quality Management (TQM) principles that gives a common sense approach to TQM as well as nine case studies that provide real-world manufacturing examples.

The Fifth Discipline (**Senge**). An eminently readable book that will give you valuable insight into cutting edge process improvement and organizational development skills. This is a great read for any JMO.

The Five Pillars of TQM (**Creech**). A valuable tool to develop your knowledge of Total Quality Concepts that continue to reshape Corporate America. Creech is a former four-star Air Force general.

The Goal: A Process of Ongoing Improvement (**E. Goldratt**). This will be one of the best business books you will ever read, and it is relevant to the military as well as Corporate America. While written as a novel, it is used as a process improvement model in organizations around the world.

How to Win Friends and Influence People (**Carnegie**). A classic book on interpersonal skills that still appears on *The New York Times* Bestseller List. Every JMO needs to read this book.

In Search of Excellence (**Peters and Waterman**). Prescribes eight principles that are in use in only the best companies. It is the #1 best-selling management book in history!

Integrity Selling (**Willingham**). A great book for anyone considering sales. Teaches an effective selling process on how to develop productive, professional and mutually rewarding relationships with customers.

Leading Self-Directed Work Teams, A Guide to Developing New Team Leadership Skills **(K. Fisher).** High performance teams are changing the business world, and Fisher's book will help you master the team leadership skills you will need to be successful in business.

Lincoln on Leadership **(Phillips).** A one-of-a-kind book that applies Lincoln's leadership traits to the business environment. This book will help you articulate your leadership experience in business terms.

Reengineering the Corporation **(Hammer and Champy).** One of the most influential books of the 90's. This concept invaded every corner of Corporate America; you <u>will</u> come in contact with its philosophies.

Results-Based Leadership **(Ulrich, Zenger and Smallwood).** A real practical book on effective leadership in the business world. Provides invaluable tools for leaders from all backgrounds.

Success is a Choice **(Pitino).** The most motivating book you will ever read by an insightful coach/motivator.

The Fast Forward MBA in Project Management **(Verzuh).** A great overview book that will help any JMO gain skills and understanding on the essential factors for successful project management.

The New Strategic Selling **(Heiman and Sanchez).** Considered the best guide for professional selling and large account management. Highly recommended by many FORTUNE 500 companies.

The Seven Habits of Highly Effective People **(Covey).** Covey's concepts are used in virtually every major corporation in America. This book is also available in an excellent 8-series tape that is narrated by Dr. Covey. You may want to read *Principle-Centered Leadership* by Covey.

World Class Manufacturing: The Next Decade **(R. Schonberger).** A must-read for all manufacturing and operations candidates. This book is required reading by virtually all forward thinking companies. You may want to read *Building a Chain of Customers*, also by Schonberger.

Appendix C

INTERVIEW SELF-EVALUATION

I strongly recommend that you evaluate your presentation before and after each interview to help immediately identify deficiencies. Companies want to hire Top Performers. You demonstrate your ability to become a Top Performer when you interview at a Perfect 10 level.

- **Before** each interview, review these key factors and focus on perfect performance.
- **After** each interview, "Rate Your Performance!" Analyze how you can improve the next time! Be critical.

When you can confidently rank at an overall Perfect Top 10 Performance Level, you are on the road to success . . . .

You can only rank yourself a 10 when each factor in the box is a 10!

Circle 5-10 (Perfect = 10)

IMPRESSION		**INTERPERSONAL SKILLS**	
• Smile	• Appearance	• Establish rapport	• Relate/Respond
• Handshake	• Walk	• Curiosity	• Connect
• Energy	• Posture/Poise	• Listen Actively	• Sincere
• Eye Contact	• FOCUS	• Approachable	• FOCUS
. . . **5 6 7 8 9 10**		. . . **5 6 7 8 9 10**	
COMMUNICATION		**CONFIDENCE**	
• Persuasive	• Body Language	• Convincing	• Knowledgeable
• Articulate	• Good Answers	• Positive	• Self-Assured
• Listen	• Good Questions	• Competitive	• Use names
• Relate Assets	• FOCUS	• Eye Contact	• FOCUS
. . . **5 6 7 8 9 10**		. . . **5 6 7 8 9 10**	

CLOSE

• Company Specific • Believable
• FOCUS
. . . **5 6 7 8 9 10**

How would you rank yourself overall?
. . . 5 6 7 8 9 10

MAKE IT A PERFECT 10!

How would the recruiter rank you?
. . . 5 6 7 8 9 10

Appendix D

SAMPLE DEVELOPMENT CANDIDATE RESUME FORMAT

John Q. Citizen
Street Address
City, State Nine Digit Zip Code
(Area Code) Home Phone Number

EDUCATION
BS Engineering/Math/Science Core Curriculum 1990
Major - Electrical Engineering
United States Air Force Academy
Colorado Springs, Colorado

AVAILABLE: March 31, 2000

MBA Finance 1994
University of Maryland
College Park, Maryland

ACTIVITIES
High School: Valedictorian; National Honor Society; County Student of Month; Rotary Club Outstanding Senior; Student of Year; Class President; Student Government Representative (Treasurer); Key Club (Treasurer, Lieutenant Governor); Alliance Area Youth Center (President); Varsity Basketball; Varsity Football; Worked part-time 6 hours per week during school and full-time 60 hours per week during summers.
College: Graduated with Distinction; National Engineering Honor Society; American Society of Naval Engineers; Habitat for Humanity (President); American Nuclear Society (Student Paper Finalist); Varsity Tennis; Intramurals (Volleyball [Captain], Football, Softball).
Note: 100% of undergraduate education financed by scholarship. 100% of graduate education financed by full-time work.

EXPERIENCE: 6/90-Present - Captain, Field Artillery, United States Army

7/94-Present Damage Control Assistant/Quality Assurance Officer: Managed maintenance and repair for all auxiliary mechanical and electrical systems on nuclear submarine, including diesel engine, hydraulic power plants, compressed air, atmospheric control, refrigeration, electronic cooling, plumbing, interior communications, and damage control equipment. Supervised 13 mechanics and 5 electricians.
• Developed new ship qualification program that resulted in 30% increase in qualification rate.
• Reengineered Quality Assurance Audit Program; new program evaluated by Nuclear Propulsion Plant Examining Board as "Outstanding" during annual inspection.
• Created new training program that resulted in receiving "Best" ship's fire drill ever seen during Operational Reactor Safeguard Examination (ORSE).

12/92-6/94 Company Commander: Led and trained a 107-person infantry company with mission to deploy worldwide on short notice to conduct combat operations. Oversaw maintenance and tactical employment of 14 Bradley Fighting Vehicles, and over $30 million worth of weapons, night vision, communications, and Nuclear, Biological and Chemical (NBC) equipment.
• Developed new maintenance program that improved equipment readiness by 5% on annual inspection.
• Implemented a relational database used for property tracking program; recognized by Command Inspection team as "Outstanding" and adopted command-wide.
• Reengineered repair parts system; resulted in an $800,000 savings of $2.1 million repair parts budget.
• Noted by Brigade Commander as #1 of 31 company commanders in Brigade.

9/91-11/92 Project Manager, Global Positioning System (GPS): Supervised a 9-member team responsible for managing work performance of 50 contractor engineers for design and verification of 33 GPS Block IIF space vehicles. Manage $900 million program budget. Planned and executed design changes. Participated in all phases of acquisition planning and request for proposal development.
• Created Integrated Product Team concept that enabled 40% reduction in government manpower.
• Forged first-ever trilateral Memorandum of Understanding between USAF, contractor, and Defense Logistics Agency, creating blueprint for revolutionized teaming concept.
• Streamlined acquisition program; contract completed 3 years early with $1 billion savings.
• Developed new concept for program reviews resulting in cutting review time from 3-4 days to 25 minutes.
• Attended 7 weeks Squadron Officer School and 4 weeks Intermediate Systems Acquisition Course.

6/90-8/91 Brigade Material Management Officer: Coordinated logistics, movement and procurement requirements for an 1,800-person signal brigade consisting of 840 wheeled vehicles and 140 major communication systems valued at $300 million. Advised commander on all logistical operations. Coordinated facility maintenance and improvements of 49 buildings worth $15 million. Supervised 9.
• Pioneered a Government Credit Card program which was adopted by Corps as example program.
• Developed first transportation method for military weapons to be moved on a civilian aircraft.
• Reduced excess equipment in brigade from 38% to 0% in 7 months.
• Co-authored a logistics article published in *Quartermaster Professional Bulletin*.
• Attended 5 months Logistics Officer Basic Course and 6 weeks Arms and Services Staff Training.

INDEX